55 Ways to the Wilderness in™
SOUTHCENTRAL
ALASKA

Helen D. Nienhueser & John Wolfe Jr.

Photographs by Nancy Simmerman

THE
MOUNTAINEERS

 Published by
The Mountaineers
1001 SW Klickitat Way, Suite 201
Seattle, Washington 98134

Published simultaneously in Great Britain by Cordee, 3a DeMontfort Street,
Leicester, England, LE1 7HD

First edition 1972, second edition 1978, third edition 1985. Fourth edition:
first printing 1994, second printing 1995, third printing 1997, revised 1998

Manufactured in the United States of America

Edited by Dana Fos
Maps by Debbie Newell and Jody MacDonald
Design and typesetting by The Mountaineers Books
Layout by Word Graphics

Fourth Edition cover photo: Hikers on Pioneer Ridge overlooking the Knik
Glacier and the inner peaks of the Chugach Mountains, trip 41 (Photo: John
Wolfe Jr.)
Title page: Golden birch, Chugach National Forest
Dedication page: (Photo: Callie Lustig)

Library of Congress Cataloging-in-Publication Data
Nienhueser, Helen.
        55 ways to the wilderness of southcentral Alaska / Helen Nienhueser
& John Wolfe Jr.—4th ed.
                p.   cm. --(100 hikes in--)
        Includes index.
        ISBN 0-89886-389-9
        1. Hiking--Alaska--Guidebooks. 2. Cross-country skiing--Alaska--
Guidebooks. 3. Boats and boating--Alaska--Guidebooks. 4. Alaska--Guide-
books. I. Wolfe, John, Jr. II. Nienhueser, Helen. 55 ways to the wilderness in
Southcentral Alaska. III. Title. IV. Title: Fifty-five ways to the wilderness of
southcentral Alaska. V. Series.
        GV199.42.A4N54   1993
        796.5'1'09798--dc20
                                                                94-5520
                                                                CIP

55 Ways to the Wilderness in™

SOUTHCENTRAL
ALASKA

Hans Van der Laan
November 17, 1937 — April 12, 1971

To Hans

Who still lives in the hearts of his family and friends and who,
through his part in this book, shares with others his love of Alaska's
mountains and valleys and his devotion to excellence.

*You cannot stay on the summit forever; you have to come down
again... so why bother in the first place? Just this: what is above
knows what is below, but what is below does not know what is above.
One climbs, one sees. One descends, one sees no longer, but one has
seen. There is an art of conducting oneself in the lower regions by the
memory of what one saw higher up. When one can no longer see, one
can at least still know.*

–Rene Daumel, *Mount Analogue*

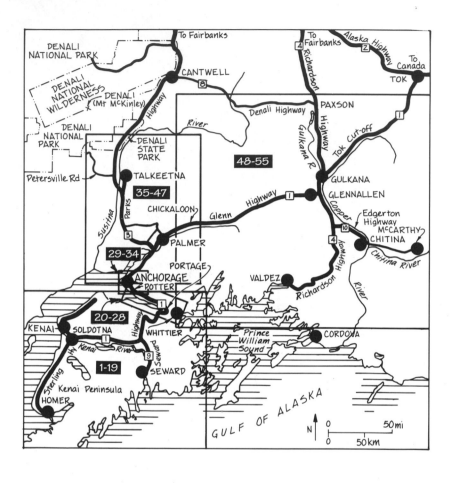

CONTENTS

ACKNOWLEDGMENTS

We thank our spouses, Gayle Nienhueser and Gretchen Nelson. We thank Nancy Simmerman for her work on previous editions. We thank those who graciously donated photographs: Gayle Nienhueser, Evan Steinhauser, Marge Maagoe, Pete Martin, Ginny Hill Wood, Susan Olsen, and Callie Lustig.

Many people accompanied us on trips, offered tips, and reviewed sections—too many to list individually. We must thank those who helped continually or provided especially substantive information for this edition: Jill Fredston, Polly Hessing, Mary Pat Brudie, Terry Slaven, Judy Reid, Lisa Oakley, Bruce Talbot, Kurt Bauer, Dan Billman, Anne Leggett, Jill Johnson, and Elizabeth Hatton.

Land management agencies were also helpful: Chugach National Forest; Kenai Fjords National Park; the Alaska Department of Natural Resources, Division of Parks and Outdoor Recreation; Kenai National Wildlife Refuge; the Bureau of Land Management; and Wrangell–St. Elias National Park.

Finally, we acknowledge the efforts of the Mountaineering Club of Alaska and its members who originally compiled *30 Hikes in Alaska* (Seattle: The Mountaineers, 1967). Bill Hauser edited that initial volume, which was the basis for the first edition of this book in 1972. Contributors to *30 Hikes* included Bob Spurr, Hans Van der Laan, John Wolfe Sr., J. Vin Hoeman, Nicholas Parker, Carol and Dave DeVoe, Gary Hansen, Rod and Gwynneth Wilson, Bill Hague, Ron Linder, and Helen Nienhueser. Most of these individuals still live in Alaska and are active in the outdoors.

PREFACE TO THE FOURTH EDITION

Changes to the Mountains

This book was first published in 1972, the year I turned ten years old. The author was (and is) my mother, Helen Nienhueser, and she inscribed a copy of that first edition for me, in part as follows:

> *I hope you enjoyed the hikes we took together when I was writing this book.... I hope there will always be wilderness for you and your children to know.*

My children? I am sure children of my own were a completely foreign concept, at that point. And what was wilderness? Like most kids, I went where my parents went and had fun sleeping in tents and tossing stones in glacier lakes (even if I did complain about yet another dumb hike). This book and its hikes just *were*. I took the book—and the wilderness—for granted.

Rereading that inscription more than twenty years later, with my own little daughter babbling babytalk in the other room, I realize how much I assume about Alaska's fine mountains. My daughter went with me up Flattop (trip 29) at one month, did her first overnight tent camping at the Gull Rock trailhead (trip 18), and completed her first three-day backpack trip at Grewingk Glacier Lake and Alpine Ridge Trail (trip 1), so history does repeat itself. But some things are not repeatable. When I was a kid, a person could scramble up Flattop or The Ramp (trip 30) on the edge of Anchorage and not only be alone but find few, if any, trails. Today, southcentral Alaska has many small trails carved out by the passage of boots. Early editions of this book touted southcentral Alaska hiking as different because there were so few trails. Now it is because there are few *maintained* trails. True wilderness is far less available to our children than it was to me.

Admittedly, this book has had something to do with the making of trackless tundra into tundra with trails. On the other hand, Alaska has millions of acres of park land now that it did not have when I was ten, and this is due to demand for parks from regular folks across the country who value wild land and wildlife and who enjoy walks in the woods—regular folks who use regular guidebooks like this one. It is people who love tundra-covered mountains blazing red in Alaska's early autumn, deep blue-green tarns, and pristine snow-covered forests who will best protect them for their children. It is our aim, in a small way, to foster that love of the country, of mountains and forests and all the plant and animal life they support, through this book.

Our biggest challenge in Alaska is maintaining the wild lands we have. Government land managers can only do so much, especially as their budgets diminish. It is up to us to protect the land we use. The term "minimum-impact camping" is now well accepted among the outdoor-oriented, but it means more than carrying out litter. It is a state of constant awareness. The phrase "leave only footprints, take only pictures" is also known, but in fragile areas, even leaving "only footprints" has caused erosion. It is up to each of us to realize that, when we hear tiny tundra roots ripping underfoot or feel trail dirt slipping, we must look for a better place for our next footstep.

Walking and wilderness are almost perversely related. We hike to find wilderness, but in hiking we leave tracks that diminish wilderness. Now that I am an author of this book, my sense of responsibility for the "55 ways" described here is heightened. My sense of responsibility for future generations is heightened, too, as I watch my daughter teeter and wobble as she learns to walk. Soon she will be hiking these trails on her own, taking both her newfound ability and the woods around her for granted, as we all do.

As grownups, we must make the effort to go consciously among the mountains. Please enjoy this book, enjoy the fine country it leads you to, and walk softly.

John Wolfe Jr.
Anchorage, October 1993

Changes in Alaska

It brings me deep pleasure to welcome my son as co-author and to share with him the preparation of this book, the love of the places we have written about, and concern for their future. His reflections on the changes to these mountains since I first took him there prompt me to reflections of my own.

The changes to the mountains have happened as a result of changes in Alaska. When I began work on the first edition of this book in the late 1960s, Chugach State Park did not yet exist, and the national parks we hike in now were more than a decade in the future. Three of the biggest changes in Alaska were the Alaska Native Claims Settlement Act in 1971, the construction of the Trans-Alaska Pipeline and the resulting flow of millions of dollars of oil revenues into state coffers, and the Alaska National Interest Lands Conservation Act (ANILCA) in 1980, which established over 100 million acres of parks and wildlife refuges.

Each of these three milestones in Alaska history represents one of three major forces that continue to weave through all facets of Alaska life: Alaska's indigenous peoples, development, and the environment. The discovery of oil at Prudhoe Bay precipitated these three milestones. Before the oil pipeline could be built, the claims of Alaska's indigenous peoples had to be addressed. And, before a workable compromise could be achieved on the Native claims, a mechanism was built into the Claims Act that led eventually to ANILCA and creation of many new parks and refuges. The battles have been fierce and divisive as Alaska has struggled to find the right balance among these three forces.

These three forces are the same forces that are at work across the globe, particularly in so-called underdeveloped nations. As these nations struggle to provide a reasonable standard of living for their citizens through development, impacts on the environment increase and protection of the environment assumes an ever-increasing urgency. And as development puts pressure on indigenous peoples, their voices rise in an effort to protect their cultures. The struggles in Alaska are very similar to struggles around the globe.

In one significant way, Alaska is very different from the developing world: our population is small—and our climate is likely to keep it that way. Because of our small population, the pressures for development are not so intense. We have a special opportunity, still, to find the right balance among these three forces. In doing so, we have the potential to be a model for others.

ALASKA FACES NEW CHALLENGES

Alaska now faces more changes, changes that will affect the areas described in this book as well as the entire state. The greatest change—and challenge—to Alaska may be shrinking state revenues. The Prudhoe Bay oil field is beginning to decline, and with it the revenues that have funded 85 percent of state government costs. We must replace oil revenues with other revenues, reduce government spending, and diversify our economy. We must work together to find the right balance between development and the environment, to seek common ground.

THE NEW ERA AND ALASKA'S WILD PLACES

Declining revenues, coupled with a worldwide rise in tourism, raise several issues for Alaska's wild places. First, as state revenues decline, funding for the state Division of Parks and other state land management agencies will decline. Second, at the same time that funding for management is declining, pressures on these wild places are likely to increase.

More tourists are coming to Alaska, drawn by our fish and wildlife, our wild places, and our scenery—increasingly rare assets in today's world. We welcome tourists for our much needed economic diversification, but they bring increased use to wild land across the state. A major challenge is to accommodate increasing use without destroying what brings the tourists here and what we love about Alaska. This means increased management costs.

In addition, as oil revenues decline there will be an intensifying search for other sources of jobs and state revenue. One result of this search will be increasing demands for revenue-generating recreational development within parks and for development of all kinds on lands that are managed for multiple use. Responding to these demands responsibly also means increased management costs. These increasing demands on the resource management agencies will likely come at the same time that their funding is being cut.

WHAT YOU CAN DO

As in developing countries, there are still many land use issues to be resolved here. Much real wilderness remains. Decisions remain to be made about whether, and if so how, our parks and wildlife refuges should be developed and how our state and federal lands outside of parks and refuges will be managed. So get involved! Because of our small population, one person can make a big difference in what happens here.

To get involved in helping agencies determine how to manage these areas or to support the agency's requests for funding, you have to know which agency manages your favorite trails. This book lists the managing agency, usually in the information block at the top of each trip description. To influence management of these areas, contact the managing agency. To support funding requests, write letters to legislators for state agencies and to Congress for federal agencies.

To understand what issues each agency deals with, you need to know what that agency's responsibilities are. The Alaska Division of Parks manages twenty-three of these "ways" for recreational use. The Division needs your support for funding to build and maintain trails, outhouses, and parking areas. Your input can help decide where there should be new trails and if and what other development should occur.

About half the "ways" in this book are on land that by law must be managed for multiple use. Chugach National Forest manages fourteen of the trails, most of which are in areas open to mining and logging. The National Forest needs your input as it tries to balance these uses and as it decides whether and where to build new trails. All or parts of twelve "ways" are managed by the state Division of Land, which also is required to manage land for multiple use.

The remaining "ways" are managed by the U.S. Fish and Wildlife Service (Kenai National Wildlife Refuge), Wrangell–St. Elias National Park, Kenai Fjords National Park, the Alaska Department of Fish and Game, and the federal Bureau of Land Management. The Appendix has addresses of these agencies and of conservation and outdoor recreation user groups.

The struggle to find the right balance for Alaska between development and the environment will continue. As we work together to find that balance, perhaps it helps to look at Alaska from a global perspective. Perhaps then our wild places will take their place among our most precious assets because they are so rare.

Help decide the future of these areas. Don't take these special places for granted!

Helen D. Nienhueser
Anchorage, October 1993

INTRODUCTION:
Backcountry Travel in Southcentral Alaska

This book is a guide to routes and trails that lead the hiker, boater, skier, and biker to some of southcentral Alaska's finest wild and beautiful backcountry. Hiking in much of Alaska is different from hiking in the more developed parts of the United States—we have fewer maintained trails. Fortunately, many of the nicest places to go are above timberline, where no trails are needed; walking is easy and pleasant on firm dry tundra. The trick, especially in southcentral Alaska, with its proliferation of brushy alder and willow, is getting above brushline.

55 Ways to the Wilderness in Southcentral Alaska describes numerous access routes to high country, making the best use of existing trails. As the population of the state grows, more trails are being built and maintained. In this book we've tried to create a pleasant balance among different kinds of trips—some through woodlands, some across tundra, a few float trips, some trips that are good for mountain biking, and several winter trips for playing in the snow.

This book also offers trips for all skill levels. The novice who has never before ventured out of the city will enjoy starting with trips 2, 20, 34, 36, and 38. The bulk of the book describes good solid trips of such beauty and variety that many of us like to redo them every few years. Some of the descriptions offer longer routes—for example, trips 48 and 51. These lead far from the road system, require a minimum of three to five days, and assume that the traveler can successfully plan and execute an extended wilderness trip.

Alternate routes and destinations are given in most of the trip descriptions. When all are tallied, this book could be more accurately titled *135 Ways to the Wilderness in Southcentral Alaska*. We suspect that many experienced Alaska hikers will find new trips here. Though each trip is field-checked every few years, conditions may differ from those described. Signs are erected or fall down, and maintenance on routes improves or is discontinued. When possible, corrections are incorporated in new printings.

Getting There

Often just getting to the trailhead is an interesting excursion in itself. Outside of the Anchorage area, Alaska's highway system is mostly two-lane roads, most of which are paved and all of which pass through wonderful scenery. A few of the access roads are not maintained or marked. Each trip description gives specific information.

Highways and primary side roads have mileposts every mile (more or less). These are often used for reference to help you locate a side road or place to park. If important mileposts were not standing, car odometers were used to estimate the mileage. Odometers were also used on side roads. Due to differing odometers, tire sizes, and reference points, our distances may vary slightly from yours, but you will be close to the trailhead and should find it with ease.

Travelers find it helpful to understand the state's system for numbering mileposts on Alaska's highways. The Glenn Highway (Alaska Route 1) and Parks Highway (Route 3) mileposts begin in Anchorage. The Richardson Highway (Route 4) mileposts begin in Valdez. The Seward Highway (Routes 1 and 9) and Sterling Highway (Route 1) mileposts start in Seward and coincide for the first 37 miles. The Edgerton Highway (Route 10) mileposts begin at the Richardson Highway.

Straightening and rerouting highways has created inconsistencies in the milepost system, with some posts closer than 1 mile and others well over a mile apart. Our figures are generally estimated from the nearest standing post.

When a road does not receive public maintenance, its condition varies greatly from year to year, with no guarantee it will be driveable. We have noted which roads might present problems. If you have doubts about whether your car can make it, don't try. Residents have become weary of pulling people out of mud holes, and getting a tow truck yourself may take hours and be very expensive. Furthermore, driving on a soft, muddy road tears it up, which is unfair to the residents who may maintain it themselves.

Following trail descriptions may also present a problem if trails are not marked or maintained. In such instances you are likely to wonder whether or not you are on the right trail, despite directions and maps. A compass is useful and so is a sense of humor if you take the wrong fork. Retrace your steps and start again. A few hikes described here follow unmarked trails that were created and are maintained only by public and animal use. Such unofficial routes can change annually. Those with limited backcountry experience should only venture into areas without marked trails in the company of more experienced companions.

A word of cheer for those who prefer well-marked, well-maintained trails—Alaska has some! Most are on the Kenai Peninsula and in Chugach State Park near Anchorage.

Trail Managers and Sources of Information

Many of the trips described here are in the Kenai National Wildlife Refuge, Chugach National Forest, or Chugach State Park. Insofar as possible, the trail descriptions are accurate, but up-to-date information can be obtained from state or federal land managers. Addresses and phone numbers are in the Appendix.

Each agency has its own regulations, designed to protect the areas it manages. In the Kenai National Wildlife Refuge and the Chugach National Forest, fire building and camping are unrestricted, although open campfires outside established campgrounds may be prohibited during times of high fire danger. Chugach State Park has few restrictions on camping but permits campfires only in established campground firepits. Chugach State Park personnel encourage backcountry travelers, for their own safety, to file a trip plan at the park office or the Eagle River Visitors Center.

The U.S. Forest Service maintains a number of cabins in Chugach National Forest for public use. Reservations must be made well in advance through any of the Forest Service offices in Alaska. A user's fee is charged for both the cabins and national forest campgrounds. Unauthorized use of the cabins is a violation of both state and federal laws and regulations, so be sure to have your permit with you.

Two publications helpful to hikers, campers, and wilderness travelers in Alaska are *Alaska's Parklands,* by Nancy Simmerman (Seattle: The Mountaineers, 1991), and *Mountaineering: The Freedom of the Hills,* edited by Don Graydon (Seattle: The Mountaineers, 1992). These volumes contain additional information about many of the topics discussed in the following sections. *A Naturalist's Guide to Chugach State Park,* by Jenny Zimmerman (Anchorage: A.T. Publishing and Printing, Inc., 1993) contains a wealth of information about the geology, plants, animals, and birds of Chugach State Park.

Hiking with Children

Which hikes are good for a child depends on the child's age, ability, experience, and attitude. Experienced Alaska hikers take their children along on almost all these trips, but some are certainly too long or difficult for the average child. Try your children on the easier hikes first. Babies can go almost anywhere in a kiddy pack, a three-year-old should be able to manage several miles a day with an occasional piggy-back ride, and children five and up can easily cover 4–5 miles a day and often more. Pick a trip that is interesting to the child, one that has a stream or lake to play in or rocks to climb on. A long, steep climb with no diversions is boring for children. Always carry water and favorite nibble foods, plus a small toy or two. There are other books available with valuable information on hiking with children. See the Appendix for suggested trips.

Equipment

Walk a short distance from the road and you may be, for all practical purposes, in the wilderness. You must be self-sufficient, with proper clothing, food, camping equipment, and navigation aids. *Mountaineering: The Freedom of the Hills* lists ten essentials to be carried at all times: extra clothing, extra food, sunglasses, a knife, matches, firestarter (e.g., candle), a first-aid kit (in Alaska, leave the snakebite kit home), a flashlight, and a compass.

On a day trip, a day pack is convenient for carrying the extra clothing and lunch. A full backpack with an internal or external frame is appropriate for overnight hikes.

Hiking cross-country is easier and safer in sturdy boots with rubber lug soles. On the other hand, heavy lug-soled boots can damage fragile terrain. Consider wearing running shoes on good trails and carry a pair with you for use in camp.

Many Alaska trails have wet stretches, and rain showers are likely. To protect leather boots from moisture, waterproof them with one of the many preparations available.

Reduce the chance of blisters by keeping boots pliable with boot grease, and always wear a pair of slippery lightweight synthetic or silk socks next to the skin under a heavier boot sock. Carry moleskin or, better, a roll of paper adhesive surgical tape (available at most drugstores), and cover any rub spots when you first notice them, not after a blister has formed.

Because southcentral Alaska's mountains often experience a rain shower or two, even on the sunniest days, many Alaskans routinely carry a lightweight rain poncho, a waterproof jacket, or a large plastic garbage bag for protection. Breathable waterproof rain gear is good for general hiking, although only truly impermeable garments will protect against day after day of deluge.

Campfires

To avoid scarring Alaska's beautiful mountains, meadows, and trailsides, do not plan to build campfires, especially in alpine areas where plant life grows so slowly. Instead, carry a backpacking stove for cooking.

Alaska is subject to disastrous forest fires in dry years. Because of the slow decay rate, peat soil layers are particularly thick; these layers will burn and a campfire may spread under the surface. It is not uncommon for such fires to smolder underground throughout the winter.

If you insist on having a campfire, please observe the following guidelines. First, to avoid creating new scars, build the fire at the site of a previous fire. Second, build it only on gravel or dirt; if a nonburnable soil is not available, do not build a fire. Third, to conserve living vegetation, use only dead trees or brush for fuel. Fourth, keep fires small. Finally, be sure to have plenty of water to extinguish the fire and, before leaving, make certain every spark is out. The infallible test is to touch the ashes carefully with bare hands. Also check the underside of any partially burned logs. Before leaving, thoroughly wet the surrounding area as well. Do not throw burning logs into a river or stream to quench them. A large forest fire was started on the Kenai Peninsula by just such a floating firebrand when it lodged against shore downriver.

Litter

All garbage and litter should be carried home. Burying garbage is not acceptable because animals will usually dig it up. In addition, the odor invites bears to investigate the campsite, endangering subsequent campers. If you have a campfire, burn paper, wet garbage, and cans, then retrieve unburned items and take them with you in a plastic bag. The volume and weight will be surprisingly small.

Sanitation

Take care to bathe, wash dishes or clothes, brush teeth, and perform toilet functions at least 200 feet away from streams and lakes. Try washing dishes with hot water and without soap. If you use soap, use a biodegradable type and pour out the used water at least 200 feet away from water sources and only into highly absorbent ground. Never use soap or detergents of any kind in lakes and streams.

Dispose of feces by burying them 6–8 inches deep and at least 200 feet from any water source. Replace the topsoil or tundra mat so the area will revegetate. Digging a new hole for each use is better for nature's decomposition system than creating a large community hole. Burn used toilet paper or carry it out with you in a plastic bag; *do not leave it on the surface of the ground!* Burn used tampons or, if that is not possible, bury them immediately and never near camp.

Minimum-Impact Camping

Hikers and backpackers create adverse impacts on the wild country they love simply by using it. The preceding guidelines will lessen those impacts. In addition, consider your effect on other users, both human and animal. Limit your group size (usually to six or fewer and not more than ten) to lessen the impact on camping areas, off-trail routes, and other users. Go quietly (except perhaps on trails frequented by bears). Leave dogs at home or keep them under control. Dogs chasing elusive squirrels are fun to watch but unhealthy for squirrels, especially be cause sooner or later the dog will catch one and kill it. Stay on trails, particularly in alpine areas, to protect fragile trailside alpine plants. Trampling vegetation leads to erosion, and scars from overuse take years to heal in the subarctic. In trailless areas with delicate plant life, spread out to avoid repeated traffic in one place. Steep areas are also vulnerable to erosion; where possible, choose a gently sloping route. Walk on rocks where possible.

When setting up camp, pick a site well away from lakeshores to avoid crowding out others and to protect water quality. When you leave, make the area look as though you were never there.

Drinking Water

It's sad but true—drinking from Alaska's lakes and streams can be dangerous. Hikers who drink water contaminated with the microorganism *Giardia lamblia* may contract the painful and incapacitating illness giardiasis, commonly known as "beaver fever." *Giardia* are carried in the feces of many mammals. Water in and below beaver ponds is particularly suspect. *Giardia* cysts survive best in cold water and could possibly be found in any surface water.

Advice differs on how to treat water to prevent giardiasis. There seems to be consensus that boiling water is the most effective treatment. *Principles and Practice of Infectious Diseases,* Third Edition

(Gerald L. Mandell, R. Gordon Douglas, Jr., and John E. Bennett, eds., New York: Churchill Livingstone, 1990, p. 2114), advises that to kill *Giardia* cysts bring water to a boil for at least one minute, and longer at higher elevations. If other contaminating organisms might be present, boil it for at least twenty minutes. This is always the safest course to be assured of 100 percent safe drinking water. To remove *Giardia* by filtration, the system must have a pore size of 0.45 microns or less. Not all hand-held backpacking filters are equally effective. Chemical methods of disinfectant are less effective for killing *Giardia* cysts, although they are effective against bacteria. Iodine-based treatments are more effective than chlorine-based treatments. Tests have shown that iodine-based treatments inactivate 99 to 99.9 percent of the *Giardia* cysts within eight hours. No chemical treatment is more than 90 percent effective at killing *Giardia* cysts with only thirty minutes' contact time.

Mosquitoes

Although generally not as much of a problem in southcentral Alaska as in the interior, mosquitoes are annoying to many people. Peak mosquito season in southcentral Alaska is the end of June and the first part of July. Mosquitoes can be thick in marshy lowlands but are rarely a problem on breezy alpine ridges.

Most Alaskans carry insect repellent during the summer, but many of these should be used with caution. Only repellents with the chemical *N,N*-diethyl-meta-toluamide (deet) have tested as effective against mosquitos, but deet is absorbed by the blood and can have side effects, occasionally serious ones. Side effects include skin irritation and neurological problems such as confusion and irritability. Also linked to the use of deet are cases of toxic encephalopathy in children, a swelling of the brain that can cause death.

Experts advise using repellents with low concentrations of deet. Some sources recommend 30 percent deet repellents, and others 40 percent for adults. Children should not use a repellent with deet concentrations higher than 15 or 20 percent. Apply deet-based repellents sparingly and only on exposed skin. Trapping the repellent under clothing can increase the possibility of side effects. Deet should not be sprayed on the face, inhaled, or ingested. Avoid putting deet-based repellents on the fingers and hands of children, so they won't swallow any of it.

Alternatives to using deet repellents on your skin include spraying clothing only, especially cuffs, collars, and waistbands, and wearing long sleeves, long pants, head nets, and even gloves. Deet is safe on cotton, wool, and nylon but may damage spandex, rayon, and acetate. Clothing treated with many deet-based repellents is also more flammable. Avoid hair sprays, colognes, and perfumes, which attract mosquitoes. Also avoid alcohol and foods high in serotonin such as bananas and nuts. Some sources recommend avoiding the use of yellow, white, and tan clothing in heavily infested mosquito areas. Some people find that frequent applications of citronella-based repellents work for them, although a test by *Consumer Reports* (July 1993, pp. 451–454) did not find these effective against mosquitoes. Oily sunscreen is said to keep mosquitos from getting a grip on your skin. Finally, stick to the ridges in peak mosquito season!

Plants

Although Alaska is free of poison ivy and poison oak, it does have a few plants that should be avoided. These include stinging nettle, devil's club, poison water hemlock, baneberry, poisonous mushrooms, and cow parsnip. The general rule of thumb is: Do not eat berries or mushrooms that you cannot positively identify as edible. Musky smelling cow parsnip is found below the alpine zone everywhere in south-central Alaska and is usually harmless, but its sap can make the skin of hikers or mountain bikers crashing through it sensitive to sun on bright days, and the resulting sunburn can lead to massive ugly blisters. Avoid this by wearing long sleeves and pants or by washing at a stream once you leave the parsnip zone. The Cooperative Extension Service (address in the Appendix) sells a useful booklet on plants: *Wild Edible and Poisonous Plants of Alaska* (1993). Other books on Alaska's plants and mushrooms are available at local bookstores.

False hellebore

Moose and Bears

One of the nicest events on an outing is seeing wildlife. Most sightings are occasions for photos and opportunities to observe the habits of Alaska's fascinating animals. Moose and bears, however, must be treated with distant respect.

Most moose will normally move away from or ignore a hiker or skier. Cow moose, however, are quite protective of their calves and can be dangerous. Expect a cow to be nearby whenever you see a calf. Stopping to take a picture is not a good idea.

Bears, either black or brown (grizzly), can be dangerous, but most will not attack humans without provocation. With sensible precautions, humans are safer in bear country than in many cities.

Although bears rarely attack, it is important to understand why they sometimes do to know how to avoid attacks. Predacious attacks are extremely rare. Almost all attacks are defensive, for one of three reasons: the bear is surprised, you are between the bear and its food source, or a female is protecting her cubs from a perceived threat.

To avoid a surprise encounter, *make noise* when traveling in bear country. This is especially important in deep brush or terrain where surprising a bear is more likely. A party of four to six people is safer than a single person because the larger group makes more noise. Whatever the size of the party, sing loudly; tie bells to your pack, waist, or boots; shake pebbles in a can or metal canteen; beat on a pot with a spoon; or blow on a noise maker. At night use a flashlight. Stick to more open routes. Walking in water along a lakeshore may sometimes be advisable because it is in the open and noisy. If the wind is from your back, you are less likely to surprise a bear.

Avoid bears' food caches and food sources. If you smell something dead and rotten, *go some other way*. If you see an animal carcass, *leave the area*. A bear may be sleeping nearby. If you see a number of magpies and eagles, they may be feeding on a bear's food cache; avoid that area. If possible, do not walk along a stream or a lake when its shore is littered with dead salmon; if you must do so, be especially alert. Be alert in berry season; berries are an important part of a bear's diet, and bears will leave salmon streams for berries.

If you encounter a bear cub, assume its mother is nearby and leave the vicinity. If the cub sees you and is curious, talk to it firmly to get it away from you. Move away slowly. Never move between a sow and her cub.

Given sufficient warning and an avenue for retreat, most bears will head away from humans. Constantly be alert for bear signs (bear trails, tracks, droppings, or diggings), and watch for the animal itself. If you spot a distant bear, avoid an encounter by changing your route or by sitting quietly (if it remains unaware of you) until it has left the area.

Camp or rest at least 25 yards away from a bear trail or salmon stream. If you cannot get that far away from a river, camp on a gravel bar in the river or in as open a spot as you can find (but be aware that rivers can rise quickly from rainstorms, including rain upstream, so be cautious in choosing a gravel bar campsite). If bear signs are abundant, reduce food odors in camp by cooking dinner in one place and then continuing another half hour before camping in another. In any camp establish a cooking area 100 yards or more from the tent. Do not keep *any* food in your tent. Cache it in a tree (16 feet above ground in brown bear country) or, if no trees are available, 100 yards or more away from the campsite. Keep all food well wrapped in resealable plastic bags. Better yet, carry and store food in bearproof containers made of PVC with screw-in caps. These are available at some sporting good stores in Alaska and fit inside many backpacks. Mothballs in small net bags (discarded panty hose work fine) attached to the outside of food caches may discourage animal raiders. Pile pots and pans on top of the food cache; if an animal gets into the cache, the tumbling pots may

Grizzly (brown) bears can run 35 miles per hour. (Photo: Patrick J. Endres)

scare it off or the noise may alert you. Do not carry especially odoriferous foods such as bacon, smoked salmon, or peanut butter. Never feed wildlife. In Alaska it is illegal to feed bears, foxes, wolves, and wolverines, either intentionally or by leaving food within their reach.

Do not wipe food off your hands onto your clothes. Before going to bed, wash your hands and face carefully and brush your teeth to remove food odors. Do not use scented deodorants, perfumes, or skin creams. Bears are attracted by any strong odor.

If, despite trying to avoid bears, you meet one, what should you do? If it has not seen you, attempt to get out of sight, giving the bear plenty of room to avoid an encounter with you. If the bear has seen you, *do not run;* running triggers a bear's chase response, and you cannot outrun a bear. Instead, let the bear know you are human. Talk to it in a normal voice. Wave your arms. Walk slowly backward, facing the bear and talking sternly, much as you would to a large, menacing dog. If the animal approaches, drop your jacket to distract it and to give you more time to get out of sight. (Do not drop your pack or anything else with food in it, as that rewards the bear.) If the bear continues to follow you, stop and hold your ground. It may just be trying to figure out what you are. Continue waving your arms and talking to the bear. Bang pots and pans or use other noisemakers.

Bears sometimes threaten with a charge but veer away at the last moment. Stand your ground, and increase your apparent size by standing shoulder to shoulder with your companions and waving a jacket. Keep talking to the bear; shouting is appropriate, but don't shriek. This usually will stop a bear from investigating further.

If, despite your efforts, the bear seems certain to attack, drop to the ground and "play dead." Don't do this until the bear actually touches you. Leave your pack on, put your hands over the back of your neck, and make no noise. This may defuse a bear's aggression. Remain motionless until the bear is out of sight and well away from the area.

On rare occasions, a bear (most likely a black bear) may perceive a person as food. If a bear bites repeatedly, it may be a predatory attack. In this case, the Alaska Department of Fish and Game recommends that you fight back vigorously.

Remaining alert and taking precautions are the most important things to do in bear country. Carrying a gun often leads to a false sense of security. Nevertheless, when traveling in bear country it's a good idea to carry something to protect yourself. Many Alaskans routinely carry guns; if you choose to do so, learn to handle it responsibly and to shoot accurately. Carry it where you can get to it to use it. The Alaska Department of Fish and Game recommends that a .300 Magnum rifle or a shotgun with rifled slugs is the most effective weapon if you know how to use it and can shoot accurately with it. Handguns may be inadequate.

If you are unable to shoot or prefer not to carry a gun, carry something else to discourage an inquisitive bear. Many Alaskans carry defensive aerosol sprays that contain capsicum (red pepper extract) and are available at sporting goods stores. These sprays may be effective at a range of 6–8 yards if there is no wind or the wind is from your back. Test the spray before leaving on your trip, but be sure the wind will not blow the spray back on you. Carry the spray can in a resealable plastic bag in a vehicle or airplane. Some people also carry noise makers (e.g., firecrackers, shriek alarms); the common highway flare used by motorists has also discouraged bears. In tents, campgrounds, cabins, and other restricted or populated situations where use of firearms would be dangerous, plan to use one of these alternatives.

Many experienced Alaskans recommend against taking an unleashed dog into the wilds; the dog may run after a moose or bear and end up being chased right back to its master. On the other hand, a well-behaved dog that can be controlled by voice is nice to have with you, as it can provide an early warning that a bear is nearby. Small, yappy dogs may irritate a bear. Pet food can attract bears.

For more information, pick up a copy of "Bear Facts: The Essentials for Traveling in Bear Country," a leaflet jointly prepared by the Alaska Department of Fish and Game and eight other resource agencies. It is available at the Alaska Public Lands Information Center in Anchorage and at wildlife management agencies.

Mountain Biking

A number of the trails in this book are open to mountain bikes, and several of the back roads used as access to trails make good mountain bike rides (see the Appendix). If the agency managing a trail has set a policy about bicycles on that trail, the description says so. If a trip description does not mention mountain bikes, the trail is not a good bicycle trip.

Mountain bikers tread a fine line. Cyclists are quiet, like hikers, but fast. They are not motorized but are mechanized, and while they usually travel "softly," they can badly erode trails. These facts leave potential for conflict with walkers, which is unfortunate but undeniable. These are among the reasons trails are closed to cyclists, and it is incumbent upon those of us who value riding in the woods and mountains and away from the road to ride responsibly and build goodwill.

To do this, avoid riding trails that are closed or not recommended for bikes. On the Kenai Peninsula, call the Seward Ranger District of the U.S. Forest Service (see the Appendix) for current trail conditions. Avoid wet trails, and try not to spin or skid. Never ride off a trail. Where there are water bars across a trail, walk the bike over the bars to avoid destroying them and to indicate your respect for the work that goes into keeping water off the trail. These measures will preserve the trail surface.

Yield to walkers as they pass head on. Mount a pleasant bike bell on your bars, and use it as you overtake walkers and as you approach corners to let people and wildlife know you are coming. Keep trail speeds down.

For your own safety, carry tools and a first-aid kit in your group and know how to use them. Regroup often with companions in case there is a breakdown in the back or someone takes a spill. Wear a helmet. Be careful not to overextend your trip and get so far off the road system that you would be overcome by darkness or exhaustion if you should have to walk back. Before going on overnight rides, load your bike and test its handling on a trail near home. On narrow, single-track trails, front panniers can be a liability, as they block views of the trail.

Boating

Alaska waters are very cold, and the waters listed for boating in this book are no exception. The Kenai River drains Kenai Lake, a natural reservoir of glacier runoff. Paxson Lake, the Gulkana River's headwaters, remains ice-covered until mid-June. Even the lakes described for canoeing are cold.

Whenever capsizing is possible, dress warmly regardless of the air temperature, and have plenty of dry warm clothes handy in a waterproof bag. A plunge into such cold water can lead to hypothermia. Know how to treat it and how to give cardiopulmonary resuscitation

(CPR). Many boaters wear wet suits for thermal protection and added buoyancy. Always wear a life jacket, even on lakes.

Be sure your boat will float even when full of water, and lash all gear securely. From shore, inspect any rapids before you float them; never attempt white water unless you have considered all possible consequences of capsizing. If you capsize, stay with the boat and work it to shore to ensure that your survival equipment is not lost.

The following river classification system, employing the International White Water Scale, has been used in this book:

WW1 (Class I) Easy. Moving water with small regular waves, riffles, and sandbars. Some maneuvering is required.

WW2 (Class II) Medium. Rapids with numerous waves up to 3 feet and wide, obvious, clear channels. Some maneuvering is required.

WW3 (Class III) Difficult. Rapids with numerous high, irregular waves capable of swamping an open canoe. A splash cover is necessary for open canoes and kayaks. Narrow passages require complex maneuvering. Scouting the route from shore is recommended.

WW4 (Class IV) Very difficult. Rapids with turbulent waters, rocks, and dangerous eddies. Constricted passages require powerful precise maneuvering, and inspection of the route is necessary. This water is normally too difficult for experts in open canoes. Boaters in covered canoes and kayaks should be able to complete an Eskimo roll.

River ratings change with water levels, some rapids becoming more difficult, some becoming easier. The rating of the upper Gulkana River, which lies far from the highway, has been increased due to the difficulty of rescue. Be particularly careful when help is far away. The presence of sweepers and snags increases the danger and may or may not be reflected in the river's rating.

Lakes present fewer obvious dangers, but their appearance can lead to complacency. Even on small, apparently calm lakes, wind can kick up white caps in a hurry. The lake trips in this book involve some portaging. Lashing a stout stick or 2x4 across the top of a large backpack as a canoe rest can make portaging easier. Portaging areas can be high-impact areas, with eroded trails and evidence of canoers' bathroom breaks. Be especially careful in these areas to take litter with you and bury feces more than 200 feet from water.

Stream Crossings

A few of the hikes described include potentially hazardous stream crossings. When confronted with such a crossing, take the following precautions:

1. Look for the widest part of the stream where the water will be the shallowest and least swift.
2. Wear boots to ensure good footing; fast streams regularly roll large rocks down their beds. If you remove your socks and keep them dry until reaching the other side, walking in wet boots will not be too uncomfortable. Some people carry old running shoes for crossings, but the foot protection is not as good.

3. Undo the waist strap of your pack for ease in getting it off should you fall.
4. Put your camera inside the pack in a waterproof sack. Its strap around your shoulders may make it impossible to remove your pack quickly.
5. Consider a rope belay from shore for each person crossing very swift water.
6. Use aids to enhance stability. By yourself, use a stick or ice ax. With companions, link arms for stability in groups of two to four, and walk in a line parallel with the current so that only one person feels the full force of the river. This technique works best if the group members all grab hold of a stick held horizontally in front of them at waist level.
7. Avoid high-water periods. If a trip will take you across glacial streams, plan the trip in early summer, or cross in early morning when water levels are likely to be lower.
8. Consider adding rocks to your pack, especially if you are small.The added weight will provide more secure footing.
9. Resign yourself to getting wet and cold, and take the crossing slowly. You are more likely to lose your balance, especially in murky glacial waters where the bottom is invisible, by leaping and jumping.

Cross large braided streams more easily by taking advantage of the stream's natural flow pattern. Take the time to scout the river and find an area with many channels. Cross from the upstream end of one gravel island to the upstream end of the next, where the water is shallower and slower due to gravel deposition. The downstream end of a gravel island where channels converge may hide a deep turbulent hole or soft sand. Try to avoid crossing toward a vertically cut bank, as such banks invariably mean the water is deepest and swiftest along that bank.

Crossing an icy river in thigh-deep water quickly saps body heat on the best of days. If it is a rainy or

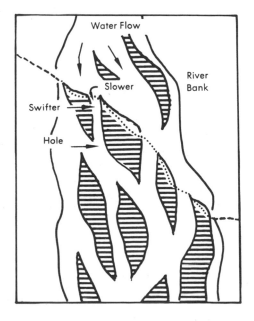

A braided stream showing gravel islands and a suggested route for crossing the stream

windy day, or if you are fatigued, the crossing could easily bring on hypothermia (see the next section). Before crossing any stream where there is danger of falling, mentally plan to avoid hypothermia. Are warm, dry clothes and sleeping bags packed in truly waterproof bags? Is there a place on each bank to set up a hasty camp should the sleeping bags and hot drinks be needed? A little forethought can go a long way in making a trip safe.

Hypothermia

Cold weather is never far away in Alaska, even in midsummer. Excessive loss of body core heat can result in hypothermia—often called *exposure*—in which the metabolic and physiological processes of the body are slowed. Death can result if body heat continues to be lost. Prevention is necessary, because you may not be able to treat a victim of severe hypothermia successfully in the field. Hikers, bikers, boaters, and skiers should always travel with extra warm clothing and high-calorie snack foods. They should monitor their bodies for exhaustion and dehydration (factors contributing to exposure) as well as temperature, and they should keep an eye on the weather. Never overextend a trip to the point that all the body's fuel stores are used up.

Cool weather, clothes and skin wet from rain or perspiration, wind, lack of food, fatigue, or poor conditioning can impose a stress on the cardiovascular system. Whenever the body can no longer meet its heat and energy needs, hypothermia begins. Falling into cold water or wearing a sweaty shirt in wind at fifty degrees Fahrenheit can easily bring on hypothermia.

Watch for the symptoms of hypothermia: uncontrollable, continued fits of shivering; vague, slow, slurred speech; memory lapses; incoherence; fumbling hands; frequent stumbling; drowsiness; and apparent exhaustion.

The victim often refuses to admit anything is wrong, so companions must insist that treatment begin immediately. To avoid further heat loss, help the victim change into dry clothing and warm layers. Find shelter from the wind. Body heat can be restored in mild cases by exercising, drinking warm liquids, and eating high-calorie foods.

When the body temperature drops below ninety degrees Fahrenheit, symptoms of severe hypothermia appear. This is a medical emergency overcome only by rewarming the body core with external sources of heat, because the victim is no longer able to generate his or her own heat. Shivering stops; the victim becomes unable to walk alone and shows poor judgment, leaving a parka unzipped or forgetting hat and mittens. Eventually, the victim may lose consciousness.

Field treatment of severe hypothermia is not always successful, but if help is far off it must be attempted. The extremities of a severely hypothermic person must not be rewarmed before the internal organs are warmed. If circulation of blood in the extremities is stimulated through massage or application of heat, that blood (which is still colder than blood in the body core) can cause ventricular fibrillation, an abnormal heart rhythm that can lead quickly to death. Ventricular fibrillation can also be triggered by moving or jarring a severely hypothermic person, so treat the victim carefully, but don't let these cautions lead to inaction. Just placing such a victim in a sleeping bag will not warm the body core, because the victim's body is unable even to warm the bag. The bag should be prewarmed by somebody else, and bottles of warm water should be placed along the victim's body core in the warm bag. The addition of one or preferably two other warm bodies in the bag is even better. Depending on how well members of the party know each other and the sexes of those involved, this may be awkward, but other bodies are the most readily available source of heat, and skin-to-skin contact speeds transfer of heat. Get medical help even if recovery seems complete; in severe cases, pneumonia or heart problems can occur later.

Before making a trip to a remote area, read the section about hypothermia in *Medicine for Mountaineering,* by James Wilkerson (Seattle: The Mountaineers, 1992). The book notes that a victim of severe hypothermia may not have a detectable heartbeat yet may still be alive. Always rewarm a hypothermia victim before assuming death has occurred.

Winter Trips

Some winter clothing and equipment are necessary for late fall and early spring travel. Carry thick mittens with windproof shells; lightweight mittens for traveling; extra wool socks; both polypropylene long underwear and warm overpants such as insulated ski pants, pile pants, or wool pants; wind pants; a warm hat; and a face mask. Pile, polypropylene, and wool fabrics are warmer, even when wet, than cotton. Gaiters, worn over boot tops, keep the snow out and help keep feet warm. To avoid condensation, clothing should not be vaporproof. If you might experience rain or wet snow, take a parka and pants of breathable but waterproof fabric.

Midwinter trips require additional equipment. A thick parka filled with down or polyester, a windproof hood, and insulated pants are recommended for day trips and mandatory on overnights. Many loose-fitting layers of clothing allow for fine-tuning body temperature at different levels of activity.

In especially cold weather, ski tourers should consider wearing either insulated overboots over ski boots or special double boots. On overnights, take mukluks and down- or synthetic-filled booties, and wear the booties inside the mukluks in camp.

In wet snow, snowshoers will be better off with insulated rubber military surplus "bunny" boots, waterproof shoepacs with a change of felt liners in the backpack, or hiking boots with insulated waterproof overboots. For cold snow (below fifteen degrees Fahrenheit), canvas or fur mukluks or bunny boots are good. Check the surplus and sporting goods stores for footgear. Be sure before leaving home that bulky boots will fit in the snowshoe binding and that the toe will move freely in the toe opening. Traditional wooden snowshoes without modern cleats will

Winter hiking on Kenai River Trail, trip 4 (Photo: Gayle Nienhueser)

travel up and down hills more easily if their frames are wrapped with polypropylene rope for greater traction.

There are all kinds of cross-country skis on the market. For touring, a light ski of medium width is usually adequate. Careful waxing or the use of "no-wax" skis make climbing skins unnecessary for general touring. No-wax skis are excellent for the changing snow conditions found on spring ski tours. On spring crusts, skating skis provide quick access to beautiful backcountry, but beware of being caught far up a wilderness valley on short, skinny skating skis in midday when the crust melts. For most of the Alaska winter, waxable skis provide the best kick and glide for general touring, even though they take longer to prepare than no-wax skis or skating skis.

For mountain touring and telemarking, heavier, wider skis with metal edges are ideal. Most skiers fasten climbing skins to the bottoms of these skis for ascending, so the stiff camber (the bow of the skis that keeps "sticky" kick wax off the snow while gliding) is not necessary. Thus, manufacturers have developed skis that perform very well descending and are used as glorified snowshoes on the way up. Because of the high performance demanded by some contemporary telemarkers, some very beefy backcountry boots are available. Although these may be perfect for lift-served ski areas, they are generally too big to be lugging around in the backcountry. Look for boots that provide lateral support and ankle support but that flex easily at the toe, are comfortable, and are relatively light.

Frostbite

At temperatures below freezing, particularly on windy days, be alert for frostbite, or freezing of body tissues. Fingers, toes, the face, and ears are normally the first to show the characteristic white patches that indicate frostbite is beginning. Windchill speeds freezing, as does direct contact with metals and other heat conductive materials. Be careful filling camp stoves in the cold, because the very cold and highly volatile gas can freeze flesh instantly. When dexterity is important—for handling cameras, ski bindings, tent poles, and the like—wear thin polypropylene gloves.

Make a habit of checking each others' faces and ears frequently, and train yourself to note the presence of sensation in your hands and feet. If feeling disappears, especially after a period of pain from the cold, immediately check for frostbite. A severely frostbitten extremity will be literally frozen, hard to the touch like meat in a freezer.

Treatment of frostbite is complicated. To prevent permanent damage to tissues or joints, it must be done correctly. Learn the prevention and first-aid treatment of frostbite before making trips at low temperatures. An excellent source of information is *Mountaineering First Aid: A Guide to Accident Response and First Aid Care,* by Dick Mitchell (Seattle: The Mountaineers, 1990).

Frost nip, the first stage of frostbite in which the surface of the skin shows white waxy patches but the underlying tissue still feels normally soft, should be treated immediately. Hold a warm hand over a frost-nipped nose, ear, or cheek to return the flesh to a healthy pink. Nipped fingers can be warmed in your armpits, between your legs, or on your stomach. Warm toes on a brave companion's stomach. Never rub a frost-nipped or frostbitten area, especially with snow.

A person with frostbite may be hypothermic, so treat accordingly, and check for further frostbite. Do not rewarm a severely frostbitten appendage in the field. Walking or skiing on a frozen foot does far less damage than traveling on rewarmed tissue. Find medical help as soon as possible.

Avalanches

If you travel through snow-covered mountains, even if only by automobile, know about avalanches. Snowslides trap or kill people every year in southcentral Alaska, but such accidents are avoidable with proper knowledge.

AVOIDING AVALANCHES

Take an avalanche awareness course through the Alaska Avalanche School (see the Appendix). Current training emphasizes not only the mechanics of snow and avalanches but the judgment of outdoor enthusiasts. Skiers not only must be constantly alert for clues to avalanche potential but also must pay equal attention to their thought processes to ensure that route decisions are based solely on these clues and not

Typical avalanche path down timbered mountainside. Upper mountain below ridge top (starting zone), blaze (track and runout zone), and nearby trees should be considered potentially hazardous in winter and spring. Although this kind of bare area on a timbered slope defines an avalanche zone, be alert for similar zones in treeless areas.

on a desire to ski an untracked slope or reach a summit, not on "gut feelings," and not on the impulsive actions of others. Winter travelers can take their clues from three things: the snowpack, the terrain, and the weather.

The snowpack is an accumulation of layers of snow from different storms, layers of ice from thaws, and layers of crystals formed within the snowpack. Snow slides when its weight becomes too much for a weak layer in the snowpack. A skier's weight may be the proverbial straw that breaks the camel's back. You may detect weak layers by hearing ominous "whumping" noises as weak layers collapse, by hearing hollow sounds, or by seeing cracks shoot through the snow from your skis. Constantly test the snow by pushing a ski pole in deep and feeling for different densities, or take a break and dig a pit to analyze the snowpack for weak layers and to see how well layers are bonded to each other.

Terrain concerns primarily slope angle. Avalanches are possible on slopes of about twenty-five to sixty-five degrees. The lower angles are the ones that most intermediate skiers love to carve turns on and even novice skiers traverse. Prime avalanche angles are thirty-five to forty-five degrees. Slope orientation, or *aspect,* is critically important. If natural avalanches are apparent on slopes facing a certain direction—say, east—or if wind is obviously depositing snow on these hypothetical east-facing slopes, beware of the east-facing slope you want to ascend. People often overlook steep spots in otherwise gentle terrain, but more than 50 percent of avalanche accidents are on slopes less than 300 feet high. Humans have triggered more than eighty avalanches on the short slope of Blueberry Hill, a foothill of sorts to Anchorage's favorite peak, Flattop Mountain. A boy in Homer was killed when he triggered the collapse of a slope only 65 feet high.

Avalanche rescue beacon practice during avalanche awareness course

Weather provides other important clues. New snow or rain add weight to the snowpack. Warming trends can quickly weaken a snowpack. Windstorms add weight in localized areas by sweeping snow off ridge crests and loading it into gullies. Even long periods of very cold weather can create an unstable snowpack by altering the crystal structure in the snowpack or can allow existing instabilities to persist.

Each member of a party venturing out in winter should wear an avalanche-victim locator beacon and be trained in its use. These battery-operated radio transceivers emit a beep audible via other transceivers. Each person should also carry a shovel and ski poles that convert to avalanche probes.

WHEN AN AVALANCHE OCCURS

Being caught in an avalanche is terrifying. Fight for your life! Yell to attract your companion's attention. Discard poles, and skis if possible, and swim vigorously to stay on the surface. As the snow slows, make an extra effort to reach the surface, and thrust an arm upward. Rescuers will find you much faster if even a finger shows above the snow. If you cannot dig yourself free, try to relax to conserve oxygen. Do not fight unconsciousness; your body needs less oxygen in that state.

If your companion is caught in an avalanche, you are the only hope. Do not send for help. The first fifteen minutes are critical. Chances of survival after thirty minutes are fifty–fifty. Few avalanche victims have been found alive after two hours. Most survivors have been rescued by people on-site when the avalanche occurred. All available hands should assist in the search.

Immediately mark the area the victim was last seen, and turn all avalanche transceivers to receive mode to avoid sending false signals. Make a quick but thorough visual search of the area below the last-seen area, and leave any discarded equipment or clothing on the surface where it was found to help mark the path. Check anything found to see if it is attached to the victim, and probe around each item.

If the initial search turns up nothing, use your avalanche transceiver for a thorough search. Without beacons, probe the snow with ski poles, skis, tree branches, anything. Check particularly areas where the snow has accumulated—above trees or rocks, at the foot of the slide, on benches or areas where the slope decreases, and on the outsides of turns. Don't endanger your own life through hypothermia, exhaustion, or additional avalanche hazard, but search as long as humanly possible. A rare few have been found alive after being buried well over four hours. If you find your companion, give CPR if necessary, and treat for hypothermia.

More thorough explanations are available in avalanche books and through workshops. One such book is *Snow Sense: A Guide to Evaluating Avalanche Hazard,* by D. Fesler and J. Fredston (Anchorage: Alaska Mountain Safety Center, 1994).

Don't let fear of frostbite or avalanches deter you. Many of us eagerly await snow. Winter is a time when rivers and swamps cease to be barriers and become highways to exciting new country inaccessible in summer. Just be aware, and ensure a safe trip.

An Invitation

We hope you enjoy using this book as much as we have enjoyed preparing it. Exploring this magnificent land and compiling the information for you has brought to us a deep appreciation for all that Alaska represents. We ask that you treat the land with respect and help others to see the value of respecting it too. Alaska has an unequalled wilderness heritage. Consider supporting the efforts of park, recreation, and conservation groups dedicated to maintaining these lands (see the Appendix). Such groups exist in nearly every Alaska community, and they are perpetually in need of volunteers.

ABOUT THIS BOOK

The trips described are arranged geographically, from Homer to Valdez. The arrangement features trips on the Kenai Peninsula first and then works its way up the Seward Highway to the Anchorage Bowl. The "North of Anchorage" section extends from Eagle River through the western Talkeetna Mountains to low foothills just south of Denali (Mount McKinley). The last section of the book explores the vast area defined by the Matanuska Valley, the upper Copper River basin, the Wrangell Mountains, and Valdez.

Each trip description includes highway directions to the trailhead, trail notes, and other information pertinent to your enjoyment of the trip. The noted hiking times are reasonable estimates for the steady but leisurely traveler who stops to enjoy the view, have a snack, and take a few pictures. Those hiking faster or slower will be able to adjust personal time estimates after just a few trips.

Total elevation gain is cumulative for all major ups and downs of the trip, thus giving you an indication of how strenuous the trip might be. Often a traverse requires less climbing if started from a specific trailhead. Elevation at key points is given throughout the text.

Distances are usually given to the nearest tenth of a mile. Where distance information is less precise, nondecimal fractions (i.e., ½) are used.

Picking the time of year when each trip is "best" or snow-free enough for use, as we do at the beginning of each trip description and in the Appendix, is sometimes difficult. The disappearance of the snowpack varies from year to year, but we've tried to choose representative dates. After a winter of heavier-than-normal snowfall, expect trails to open at least two weeks later than indicated. May is a tricky month in Alaska. At the lower elevations summer has arrived, but above 3,000 feet winter weather dominates. For trips above 3,000 feet, take winter equipment. An easy climb in summer may call for a rope under winter conditions.

Hiking is usually good through September everywhere in south-central Alaska; below 3,000 feet, trails may be snow-free well into October. In areas of light snowfall, trips near sea level often may be walked throughout the winter.

The river gradient is listed for float trips. The number of feet of elevation lost per mile is one element that helps determine the difficulty of the river. The white water ratings are another, more comprehensive, indicator of difficulty.

The maps accompanying every trip description give important information of interest to the hiker, skier, mountain biker, or boater, but they should not be used for routefinding. The following subsection describes maps in more detail.

Maps

The maps in this book were made as overlays of U.S. Geological Survey (USGS) topographic maps. Although it was often necessary to change the scale of the maps to make them fit in the book, you can be assured that relationships between features are to the scale indicated on each map. These are not just "sketch maps," but this does not mean they show enough detail for travel.

These maps are designed to be used with USGS topographic maps. Using the book's maps, locate the route on the appropriate USGS maps listed at the top of each route description. The combination of the two types of maps will give you far more information than either map separately. Carry and know how to use USGS maps; without their information you could become lost within a short distance of the road system. With the topographic maps, you will understand what lies ahead of you

Consulting topographic maps, trip 48 (Photo: John Wolfe Jr.)

on the trail and be able to plan your own routes and side trips.

Recently, the USGS has been dividing each standard southcentral Alaska map into four separate maps. For years the standard has been maps at a 1:63,360 scale (1 inch equals 1 mile). These are designated with a quadrangle number, like "Anchorage A7" or "Seward D8." The new maps are based on the original inch-to-the-mile maps but, at 1:25,000 scale, show much more detail. These newer maps—northwest, northeast, southwest, and southeast divisions of the original quadrangles—are sometimes cumbersome to use. This is especially true where the USGS has the new maps for some areas but not for adjacent areas.

For some hikes using the new maps means dealing with four maps, whereas using the original maps requires only two. Priority areas for making the new maps have been along roads, which sometimes leaves hikers with maps at one scale near a trailhead and another scale back in the sticks. Also, the new maps are somewhat cumbersome because they give elevations only in meters, and the elevation points thus do not match the original maps for comparison. The new maps do, however, show the most up-to-date roads and trails. While the original maps will continue to be available, they may not show the roads leading to trailheads.

This book lists the appropriate USGS 1:63,360 map number (e.g., "Anchorage A8"), and if that map had been subdivided by this book's publish-

LEGEND FOR MAPS IN THIS BOOK

Start of Trip	●	Campground	▲
Trail	▬ ▬ ▬ ▬ ▬	Point of Interest	◇
Secondary Trail	— — — — —	Pass	] [
Route (when no trail exists, generally above timberline)	• • • • • • • •	Text Reference	◇1
		Building	⌂
Secondary Route	· · · · · · · · · · · ·	Town or Community	●
Major Road	▬▬[1]▬▬	Powerline	— — I — — I — —
Minor Road	▬▬▬▬▬	Land Unit Boundary	—·—··—··—··—··
Unmaintained Road	＝＝＝＝＝:	Stream and River	
Trail Along Unmaintained Road	▬▬▬▬▬▬	Lake or Body of Saltwater	
Railroad	┼┼┼┼┼┼┼┼┼┼┼	Mountain Summit	x 6,119'
		Glacier	

ing deadline, this book lists the appropriate 1:25,000 map (e.g., "NW"),
Note that if a hike calls for "Anchorage A7 NW," you can purchase Anchorage A7 at 1:63,360 or the Anchorage A7 NW map at 1:25,000.

Whichever you choose, never travel off the beaten path without USGS maps. Note that magnetic north, as read from a compass, and true north differ significantly in Alaska, and know how to correct for the difference. Addresses of the USGS map sales office is listed in the Appendix. A guide to symbols used on the USGS topographic maps is also available from the sales office. Symbols used on maps in this book are outlined in the legend above.

The Authors

A Note About Safety

Safety is an important concern in all outdoor activities. No guidebook can alert you to every hazard or anticipate the limitations of every reader. Therefore, the descriptions of roads, trails, routes, and natural features in this book are not representations that a particular place or excursion will be safe for your party. When you follow any of the routes described in this book, you assume responsibility for your own safety. Under normal conditions, such excursions require the usual attention to traffic, road and trail conditions, weather, terrain, the capabilities of your party, and other factors. Keeping informed on current conditions and exercising common sense are the keys to a safe, enjoyable outing.

The Mountaineers

KENAI PENINSULA

Opposite: *Russian River Cascades, July*

1 GREWINGK GLACIER AND ALPINE RIDGE

GREWINGK GLACIER LAKE
Round trip: 6.5 miles
Hiking time: 3–5 hours
High point: 158 feet
Total elevation gain: 158 feet
Best: May to October
USGS map: Seldovia C4 NE, SE

Kachemak Bay State Park

ALPINE RIDGE
Round trip: 5 miles or more
Hiking time: 4.5 hours to 2 days
High point: 2,000–4,050 feet
Total elevation gain: 2,000–4,050 feet
Best: June to September
USGS maps: Seldovia C3; C4 NE, SE

Kachemak Bay State Park offers hikes for everyone—from families with infants to experienced backpackers—and even the easiest comes complete with a glacier lake, icebergs, towering peaks, and a spectacular coast. The most accessible routes lead to a large lake at the foot of Grewingk Glacier and to a high ridge overlooking the lake, the ice, and the ocean.

The park, across Kachemak Bay from the city of Homer, requires boat or airplane access. Water taxis and air taxis are available in Homer. Experienced ocean kayakers can cross the bay but only on the calmest days. Water taxis can carry kayaks on other days.

Homer is at the end of the Sterling Highway, 226 miles south of Anchorage. Follow the main highway and signs for Homer Spit, a narrow 4-mile peninsula that juts into the bay. The small boat harbor and water taxis are near the end of the spit. A visitor information cabin, 3½ miles out the spit on the right, near a camping area, can help locate a water taxi.

The state park trail system starts from Halibut Cove (the actual cove, not the community), 8 miles across the water from Homer Spit. Beachfront trailheads are designated by orange markers.

Grewingk Glacier Lake

The trail to Grewingk Glacier Lake begins at the Glacier Spit trailhead. Glacier Spit is a 2-mile tongue of gravel north of Halibut Cove. The trail actually begins well south of this long landmark spit and just north of a shorter spit enclosing Rusty's Lagoon. Along this easy 3.2-mile path, take a ¼-mile detour on a nature trail established by a Homer Eagle Scout, and learn about the surrounding glacial landscape. The trail passes a cutoff that leads to a tram crossing of the Grewingk River and a second cutoff for Saddle Trail. Beyond the second cutoff, the route is marked with cairns, but these rock piles may be difficult to pick out at first against the background of glacial cobbles. At the lake's broad beach, campsites abound. Camp away from the water to avoid tying up the beach for others.

Drinking water is an issue for camping. The lake is glacial; the silty water is drinkable but not appealing. Let it settle as much as possible and skim off the clearer water for boiling before consumption. (The silt will quickly clog a water filter.) A better bet is to melt icebergs for water. Take an ice ax or other chipping tool to break ice into pot-sized chunks, and be prepared to take a step or two into the icy water to reach a grounded berg. A small stream at the Saddle Trail junction also is a possibility for water.

This area could be easily ruined by insensitive use. Find and use the toilet provided near the lake.

Another camping option is to use the park's established hike-in campsite located on Rusty's Lagoon, less than a mile from the Glacier Spit trailhead. From there, the lake is an easy day hike.

Alpine Ridge

The quickest access to Alpine Ridge Trail is from the Saddle Trail beachhead. Saddle Trail also provides a steep 2-mile route to Grewingk Glacier Lake. Known by local hikers as the stairway to heaven, the climb up Alpine Ridge Trail allows access through the forest and brush to spectacular alpine country. The ridge crest, which parallels Grewingk

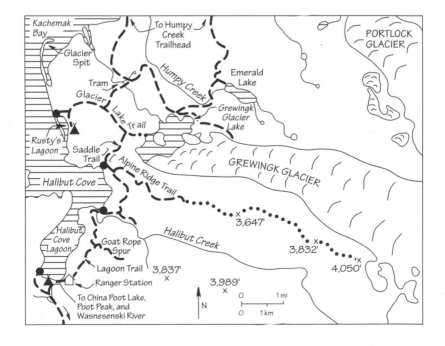

39

Glacier for more than 7 miles, consists of rolling tundra knobs interspersed with tiny ponds. It provides views across the mile-wide glacier and the much larger icefield that feeds it.

From the beginning of Saddle Trail on the east side of Halibut Cove, climb steeply about 400 vertical feet to a trail intersection at a saddle in the ridge. The saddle may also be attained from Glacier Lake Trail, as already described. At the saddle, a sign points the way to the Alpine Ridge and Lagoon trails. Follow this fork a short way to another fork. Go left to reach the ridge. The large Sitka spruce and the thick green understory create a different forest than is found along most trails in southcentral Alaska and make for pleasant walking. The trail has few flat spots, however, and because the forest is thick, few vistas are available until the trail breaks into meadow and brush about 1¼ miles from the saddle at about 1,400 feet. Conveniently, the trail levels briefly in this area and invites a rest.

Continuing upward, the trail enters the alpine zone, where the ridge again levels off, this time at a series of knobs and pocket-sized valleys. Camping is possible here, although water may be scarce after the last snow patches melt in mid- to late June. Pond water should be purified by boiling, filtering, or treating. Continuing up the ridge toward point 3647, which is 3.5 miles from the saddle, the well-worn path eventually peters out, but the ridge may be walked to at least point 4050. The views increase with the elevation.

Grewingk Glacier from Alpine Ridge Trail, May (Photo: John Wolfe Jr.)

Other Trails

The Alaska Division of Parks has been expanding this trail network. The Lagoon Trail, which forks off the Alpine Ridge route, is difficult but provides access to miles of trail south of Halibut Cove Lagoon. A tram across Grewingk Creek leads to an Emerald Lake loop trail. Call the visitor information center or the Division of Parks in Homer (phone numbers in appendix) for updated information on trails and transportation across the bay.

2 HOMER BEACH WALK

Round trip: 4 miles or more
Hiking time: 1–8 hours
High point: sea level

Elevation gain: none
Best: anytime
USGS map: Seldovia C5 NE

Kachemak Bay State Critical Habitat Area, Alaska Department of Fish and Game

A delightfully different Alaska experience, summer or winter, a walk along the Homer beach takes you away from the bustle of the town. Kachemak Bay, with its mountain backdrop, is one of Alaska's loveliest areas.

On the beach at low tide, look for sea stars (starfish), many kinds of clam shells, mussels, whelk (neptune) shells, rocks covered with barnacles, sea urchins, snails, crabs, small shorebirds, gulls, and kittiwakes. Coal and sometimes fossils can be found below the cliffs that border the beach. Waterfalls cascade to the beach; driftwood logs thrown up by storm waves provide ready benches and tables for picnics. Walkers of all ages, from toddlers to grandparents, will enjoy a walk in the brisk salt air.

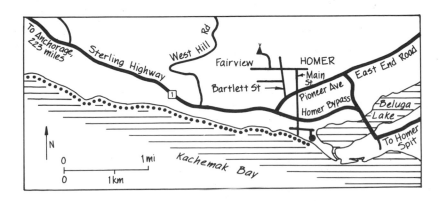

Beach at Homer, May (Photo: Helen Nienhueser)

At low tide a broad sandy beach extends oceanward. High tides cover the sand, forcing the hiker onto gravel and rocks near the base of the cliffs. Consult tide tables, available from most gas stations and banks, before setting out.

Pick a day with a reasonably low tide and schedule the walk to leave before low tide, returning to Homer well before the tidal high. The highest tides come in all the way to the cliffs, a potential hazard. In some places the cliffs cannot be climbed, and the highest tides could trap the unwary. However, watch the hour and you'll have no problems. Wear rubber boots or well-greased hiking boots; many little inlets left behind by the retreating water must be crossed. Don't be caught as the tide pours back into these inlets, turning peninsulas into islands.

Homer is a charming seaside community at the end of the Sterling Highway, 226 miles south of Anchorage. To reach the beach, drive to the bottom of the Sterling Highway hill as it enters Homer. From the intersection with Pioneer Avenue, which leads to the business district, proceed straight on the Homer Bypass. In 0.2 mile, turn right on Main Street. Take the first left, Bunnell Avenue, and then the next right, Beluga Street (follow signs for "Beach Access"). This street ends in a parking area for Bishop Beach Park.

Wander the beach to the west as far as time permits. A good destination, an hour's walk away, is the rocky spit about 2 miles from the parking area. Extending far out into the water at low tide, this spit offers excellent beachcombing. Shortly after low tide, this spit is covered by water, so plan your walk accordingly, allowing more time if you beachcomb en route.

At very low tides, good beachcombing is also available on the east side of the base of Homer Spit, at Mud Bay. Park on the spit road about a mile south of Kachemak Drive (the road to Homer's airport) and walk out to the tidal flats.

Camping is available in the city campgrounds on the hill above town (access from Bartlett Street) and on the spit for a fee.

3 SWAN LAKE AND SWANSON RIVER CANOE ROUTES

SWAN LAKE
Up to 60 miles
Allow 2 days to 1 week
River gradient: 4 feet/mile
Best: May to early October
USGS maps: Kenai C2 NW, NE;
In addition, for Moose River,
Kenai C2 SE, SW; C3 SE

SWANSON RIVER
Up to 80 miles
Allow 2 days to 1 week
River gradient: 4 feet/mile
Best: late May to early October
USGS maps: Kenai D1 3W; D2 SE,
SW; D3 SW; C2 NW; C3 NE, NW

Lowland Wilderness Unit, Kenai National Wildlife Refuge

A long chain of lakes, streams, and rivers in the wooded northwestern Kenai Peninsula offers good, safe canoeing and kayaking. Rough water is seldom a problem because most of the lakes are small and the rivers placid. Portages are well marked and well cleared, and most are short. Take 2 days or 2 weeks—many route variations are possible. More time means more fun exploring and fishing. A rich variety of water birds inhabit these waters, including many species of ducks and shorebirds, loons, snipes, and swans. Anglers will find rainbow trout, Dolly Varden, steelhead trout, and landlocked salmon. Watch for moose, beavers, muskrats, and bears. In winter the canoe trails offer good ice skating and ski touring.

The Swan Lake and Swanson River canoe routes are two separate systems. Both are reached from mile 83.5 of the Sterling Highway, 1.4 miles west of the Moose River bridge (136 miles south of Anchorage). (The Izaak Walton State Recreation Site beside the bridge is an exit for the Moose River extension of the Swan Lake Canoe Route.)

At mile 83.5, turn north onto Swanson River Road (Robinson Loop Road). Expect no automobile fuel beyond here. About 17 miles from the Sterling Highway is a junction with Swan Lake Road. Swanson River Road continues north 0.6 miles to the Swanson River and a campground. This is an exit for the Swanson River Canoe Route.

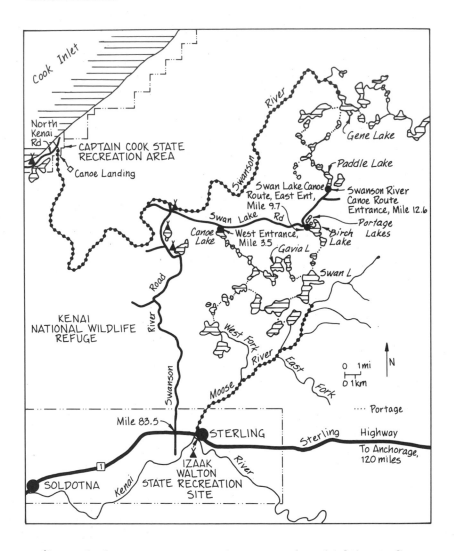

To reach the canoe route entrances, turn east (right) onto Swan Lake Road. The Swan Lake Canoe Route lies south of the road; the Swanson River Canoe Route lies north of it.

The Swan Lake system has two entrances, the west entrance at Canoe Lake, mile 3.5 of Swan Lake Road, and the East Entrance at Portage Lakes, mile 9.7. From either entrance the canoeist can reach Moose River and float it to the Sterling Highway bridge. This trip can be done in 2 long, hard days, but more time is recommended for most people, especially for those not experienced at portaging boats and gear. Expect to reach Gavia Lake late the first day from either entrance (it is closer to the west entrance). Plan to take several hours from Gavia Lake to Swan Lake, and at least 6 hours to portage from Swan Lake to Moose River and paddle to the bridge. Camping along the Moose River during the first 1½ hours is poor. An easier 2-day trip is from one entrance to the other via Gavia Lake. Many other variations are possible. Strong winds can create whitecaps and difficult-to-dangerous canoeing on Swan Lake because it is so large. There are nice mountain views from Gavia, Konchanee, Cygnet, and Swan lakes.

The Swanson River Canoe Route entrance is at mile 12.6 of Swan Lake Road, at Paddle Lake. From there explore various routes through the lakes or take a 2–3-day trip through a series of lakes and out Swanson River. To reach the river, head north to Gene Lake (1 day) and then down Swanson River for 12–14 hours to the campground at the north end of Swanson River Road.

Another exit about 12 hours farther is near the mouth of he Swanson River at Captain Cook State Recreation Area. Highway access is from the city of Kenai. Drive to mile 38.5 of North Kenai Road, and follow a side road south to reach the canoe landing.

Before setting out, check the Swanson River water level with the Kenai National Wildlife Refuge office (address in the Appendix). Low water can make the first several miles of the river nearly impassable as it flows sluggishly through muskeg and dense masses of lily pads. The small stream connecting Gene Lake and Swanson River generally requires lining the boats and includes two short portages. A campsite can be found at the end of the second portage. Most campsites along the river are some distance from the riverbank through muskeg and marsh.

Gavia Lake, Swan Lake Canoe Route, June

Good primitive campsites are available at most lakes in both systems. Build fires only on bare dirt in existing fire pits, not on moss or peat, and be sure to pour a lot of water on the fire and surrounding earth when you are finished. Campfires may be restricted in dry years. Cutting green trees is prohibited. Consider using a camping stove in this popular area. Wear rubber boots because lakeshores and portages are often wet and boggy.

A brochure with maps showing the canoe routes is available from the refuge manager and usually at the trailhead and at the refuge visitor center at mile 58 of the Sterling Highway. These maps are extremely helpful in locating connecting channels and portages, both of which are marked with small, unobtrusive brown signs that are difficult to see from a distance.

Canoes can be rented in Anchorage, Soldotna, and Sterling (addresses in the Appendix). Guided trips are available. The Swan Lake and Swanson River canoe routes are part of the National Trail and National Wilderness systems. No wheeled or motorized vehicles are permitted within the canoe route areas; this includes powerboats, snowmobiles, aircraft, off-road vehicles, mountain bikes, and wheeled canoe carriers.

HIDDEN CREEK AND KENAI RIVER TRAILS

HIDDEN CREEK TRAIL
Round trip: 3 miles
Hiking time: 2–3 hours
High point: 500 feet
Total elevation gain: 0 feet in, 300 feet out
Best: May to October
USGS map: Kenai B1 NW

KENAI RIVER TRAIL
Round trip: 8 miles
Hiking time: 4–6 hours
High point: 550 feet
Total elevation gain: 300 feet northbound, 150 feet southbound
Best: May to October
USGS map: Kenai B1 NE

Kenai National Wildlife Refuge

A pleasant, easy trip for the whole family, Hidden Creek Trail winds to the shore of Skilak Lake near the mouth of Hidden Creek. Watch for spruce grouse, moose, coyotes, wolves, and bears. At the lake, fish for rainbow trout, lake trout, Dolly Varden, silver and red salmon, and whitefish.

At mile 58 of the Sterling Highway (111 miles south of Anchorage), turn south onto Skilak Lake Road, marked by a sign for Skilak Wildlife Recreation Area. Drive 4.7 miles; the trailhead is marked. Park in the area provided across the road.

Hidden Creek Trail starts at 500 feet elevation and descends

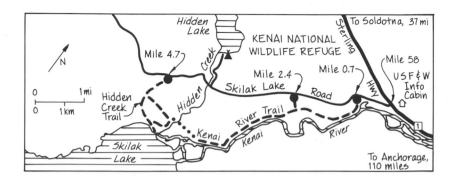

through pleasant woods to Skilak Lake at 195 feet elevation. The trail quickly drops into wet meadows and lush coniferous forest. Logs have been laid across the trail to make walking drier, but there are still wet sections. Continue through a forest of evergreens and birch trees protecting a forest floor covering of moss, cranberry, crowberry, and Labrador tea. The trail forks about halfway in. Both trails end at the shore of Skilak Lake. The left-hand (east) fork is about half a mile

Skilak Lake near Hidden Creek

47

longer but is in better condition. It goes past Hidden Creek. The right-hand (west) fork goes directly to the lake where an endless supply of driftwood invites log-hopping and photographs. A short walk to the east along the lakeshore is the mouth of Hidden Creek. Lovely mountain vistas grace the horizon. Campers should prepare for possible strong winds near the lake (be careful with campfires during these conditions).

Kenai River Trail, marked at the road, leaves Skilak Lake Road 0.7 mile from its east junction with the Sterling Highway (elevation 300 feet). The trail heads down an old dirt road 0.2 mile to the river, then uphill to the south and more or less parallels the river downstream for a little less than 4 miles before it disappears. There are good views of the Kenai River canyon from the first part of the trail. Another access to the trail is at mile 2.4 (elevation 700 feet). Round-trip distance via this access is about 5 miles. The May 1991 Pothole Lake fire opened up many scenic vistas from this access. A loop trip is possible from this access (see map). The southern part of the loop follows the river and cuts through interesting sections of the Pothole Lake Fire—a lot of fireweed, cow parsnip, lupine, and other plants that grow well after a fire. Much of the north part of the loop goes through grassy meadow and burn areas.

It is possible to go from the end of Kenai River Trail to Hidden Creek Trail or vice versa. The route crosses Hidden Creek about ¼ mile upstream from Skilak Lake. When the creek is high, it is difficult to cross. The route between the two trails is about ½ mile long across a marshy area and may be very wet. Experience with map reading and routefinding is necessary to go from one of these trails to the other.

These trails and the Kenai River gravel bars make good ski or snowshoe trips, although in winter Skilak Lake Road may not be plowed. Where the river does not freeze over, watch for wintering bald eagles.

The trails are closed to off-road vehicles, including snowmobiles and mountain bikes, all year.

5 SKILAK LOOKOUT

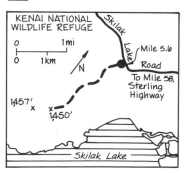

Round trip: 5 miles
Hiking time: 3–4 hours
High point: 1,450 feet
Total elevation gain: 750 feet
Best: May to October
USGS map: Kenai B1 NW

Kenai National Wildlife Refuge

The trip to Skilak Lookout offers an easy-to-find trail through pleasant spruce and cottonwood forest with a lovely view at the end. This is a moderately difficult trip that is good for children who can walk 5 or so miles. Watch for spruce grouse, moose, and bears.

At mile 58 of the Sterling Highway (111 miles south of Anchorage), turn south onto Skilak Lake Road (marked by a sign for Skilak Wildlife Recreation Area). Drive to mile 5.6; the trailhead (elevation 700 feet) is marked. Parking is on the opposite side of the road.

Skilak Lookout Trail leaves the south side of the road and climbs gently through pleasant woods. A few spots on the trail may be wet. Exposed tree roots abound, and it may be necessary to go around or over a few fallen trees. Occasional glimpses of Skilak Lake appear. In August raspberries line the trail and might attract bears as well as hikers. Make plenty of noise during berry season to avoid surprising a bear.

Near the end, the trail climbs steeply to a knob (elevation 1,450 feet) and is slippery when wet. A 1996 fire affected this area. From the knob, view Skilak Lake, the Kenai Mountains, Mount Redoubt volcano to the west, and Mount Spurr and Mount Gerdine to the northwest. The view is worth the trip, even in misty weather.

There are no developed campsites here, but seven public campgrounds are located along Skilak Lake Road. The trail is closed to off-road vehicles, including snowmobiles and mountain bikes, all year.

Skilak Lake from lookout, May

6 FULLER LAKES

FULLER LAKE
Round trip: 6 miles
Hiking time: 4–7 hours
High point: 1,690 feet
Total elevation gain: 1,400 feet in,
  35 feet out
Best: June to October
USGS maps: Kenai B1 NE, C1 SE

TRAVERSE
One way: 12 miles
Hiking time: 12 hours to 2 days
High point: 3,520 feet
Total elevation gain: about 5,400
  feet, either direction
Best: June to September
USGS maps: Kenai B1 NE, C1 SE

Mystery Creek Wilderness Unit, Kenai National Wildlife Refuge

Fuller Lake, a tempting jewel, lies at timberline surrounded by scattered hemlock, spruce, willow scrub, and grassy meadows. Lower Fuller Lake, smaller and nestled just below timberline, is a good destination for families.

Hikers can make Fuller Lake their goal or continue up the ridge to the west for a panoramic view. Really energetic hikers may want to follow the ridge of the Mystery Hills over its various summits to Skyline Trail, which descends to mile 61 of the Sterling Highway.

To reach the lakes, drive to mile 57.2 of the Sterling Highway (110 miles south of Anchorage), and park in the parking area on the north side of the highway (elevation 300 feet).

The trail begins up a set of steps from the parking lot. Follow this trail

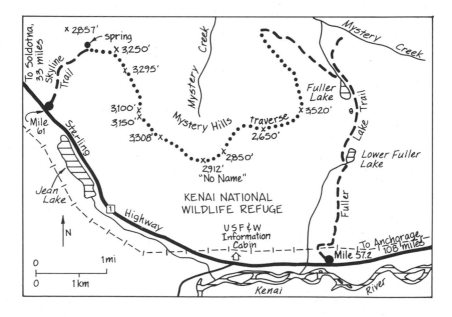

Lower Fuller Lake, August (Photo: Helen Nienhueser)

north as it climbs through forest and meadows. Look back frequently for views of Skilak Lake and the mountains to the southeast. This is a moderately difficult hike. Most of the elevation is gained between the trailhead and Lower Fuller Lake. Exposed tree roots and occasional fallen trees across the trail may be encountered along the way.

At Lower Fuller Lake cross the outlet stream (normally easy), and continue along the left side of the lake and over a low pass to Fuller Lake, an ideal overnight spot. The lakes are actually in different drainages; Fuller Lake drains north into Mystery Creek and Lower Fuller Lake drains south into the Kenai River. The wood supply at Fuller Lake is limited; use a backpacking stove rather than a fire.

Ridges and knobs beckon from Fuller Lake; brush presents little obstacle to exploration. The trail continues around the east side of the lake and then branches into a confusion of small trails. A right branch continues a short distance north, about 4.8 miles from the trailhead, before disappearing. A left branch leads up onto the ridge west of the lake to become the traverse (not maintained).

To reach the ridge, cross the outlet of the lake and find a trail that heads northwest, traversing gradually away from the lake and up and across the side slope of the 3,520-foot summit of the Mystery Hills on the west side of the lake. This trail goes to the base of the north ridge of the mountain. Follow this ridge to the summit for the least-steep route to the top. A one-day traverse is best done in late June or July when there is plenty of light. People have been caught by darkness here. Hiking the entire ridge traverse is a long, very strenuous

1-day trip, with nine "summits" to climb over. A high meadow and spring at the western end offer a possible campsite, but otherwise snowbanks provide the only water. Above brushline, the route is unmarked.

The traverse joins Skyline Trail, which is 1¼ miles long. It leaves the north side of the Sterling Highway just east of mile 61. The sign for the trailhead (elevation 450 feet) is on the south side of the road. Park here; the trail begins on the north side of the guard rail. Skyline Trail is maintained but climbs very steeply, and footing can be slippery.

This area is included in the National Wilderness System. Off-road vehicles (including mountain bikes) are not permitted during snow-free months, and snowmobiles are prohibited above timberline in winter.

7   KENAI RIVER

Kenai Lake to Upper Skilak Lake Campground: 19 river miles plus 6 lake miles
Allow 1 day
River gradient: 14 feet/mile
Best: May to October
USGS maps: Seward B8; Kenai B1 NE, NW

Lower Skilak Lake Campground to Kenai: 50 miles
Allow 1 or 2 days
River gradient: 4 feet/mile
Best: May to October
USGS maps: Kenai B2 NE, NW; B3 NE, NW; C2 SW; C3 SE, SW; C4 SE

Kenai River Special Management Area; Alaska Division of Parks and Outdoor Recreation and Kenai National Wildlife Refuge

A good trip for rafters and for the intermediate or experienced canoeist or kayaker, the Kenai River offers just enough white water to be

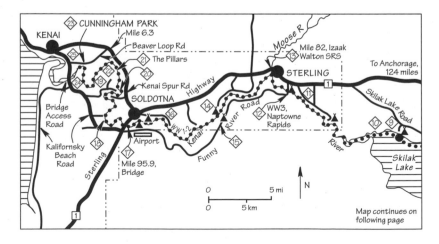

Map continues on following page

interesting. Caution is required because of swift, cold water and rapids.

After flowing from turquoise, mountain-rimmed Kenai Lake (elevation 436 feet), the river runs 19 miles to Skilak Lake. It then continues to its end on the coastal flats of Cook Inlet, at the city of Kenai. The section above Skilak Lake, with its steeper gradient and relatively undeveloped shoreline, is more popular with floaters. Below Skilak Lake, the river is congested with powerboats and shoreline development. The shores abound with migrating and nesting birds. In autumn and early winter, bald eagles, attracted by a late salmon run, perch on trees beside the river.

Numerous entrances/exits for this trip make many variations possible. A good trip, of medium difficulty (WW2), is from the entrance at Cooper Landing (1) to Jim's Landing (4), 13 river miles. This section has one set of WW3 (difficult) rapids at Schooner Bend (2); for the calmest water, travel against the right bank. (Classifications of river difficulty are described in the Introduction.)

For experienced boaters, a longer 1-day trip, which includes the Kenai River canyon, goes from the entrance at Cooper Landing (1) to Hidden Creek Trail (7), 19 miles, or Upper Skilak Lake Campground (8), 6 miles farther along the lakeshore. The canyon has 2 miles of WW3 rapids. Experience is necessary as are splash covers for canoes and kayaks. While the white water is good for rafts, note that it is a long way to row across the lake and not easy to carry a raft up Hidden Creek Trail. Guides take along a small outboard for use on the lake.

From Skilak Lake (9) (elevation 195 feet) to the city of Kenai boat harbor (25), 50 river miles, the river is rated WW2 or less except for a single stretch of WW3 at Naptowne Rapids (12). Cunningham Park is a good exit. From mid-April to early May, however, the trip through the Kenai River Flats, all the way to the City of Kenai boat harbor, is great for bird-watching. The Flats are on a major migration route for many species of waterfowl including snow geese, sandhill cranes, swans, and

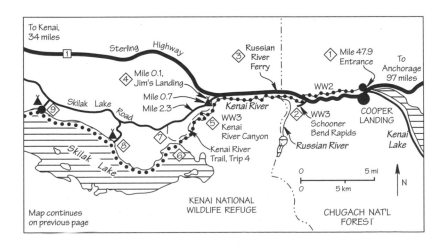

many geese and ducks. Please enjoy the birds from your boat and do not disturb them by going onshore. The Kenai River Road and Recreation Map (Skilak Lake to Cook Inlet, 1:25,000) is a convenient map to use for this trip; it is available at grocery stores and bookstores.

Boats may be portaged or lined around all rapids except those in the Kenai River canyon. Skilak Lake is subject to high winds that swiftly whip up large waves and can therefore be dangerous. A number of lives have been lost when boats have overturned. Always stay close to shore, and stay off the lake in rough weather.

The first entrance is Cooper Landing at mile 47.9 of the Sterling Highway, 101 road miles south of Anchorage. From here it is 19 river miles and 6 lake miles to Upper Skilak Lake Campground and 76 river miles to the boat ramp at the city of Kenai's Cunningham Park. Major points of interest along the way are keyed to the map:

(1) Entrance, .1 mile west of Kenai River bridge, mile 47.9 of the Sterling Highway; parking fee.

(2) Schooner Bend rapids (WW3) immediately after a highway bridge.

(3) Exit/entrance, Russian River ferry and boat launch; parking fee.

(4) Exit/entrance, Jim's Landing boat launch; a short side road leads to mile 0.1 of Skilak Lake Road.

(5) Kenai River canyon, 2 miles of WW3 rapids.

(6) Skilak Lake, about 3 miles below the canyon.

(7) Exit, Hidden Creek Trail (trip 4) to Skilak Lake Road, 1.5 miles away by foot.

(8) Exit, Upper Skilak Lake Campground, 6 water miles along the lakeshore from the Kenai River; highway access, 10 road miles from mile 58 of the Sterling Highway via Skilak Lake Road.

(9) Entrance, Lower Skilak Lake Campground, 6 miles by water from upper campground; 45 miles to Cunningham Park; highway access, 16 miles from mile 58 of the Sterling Highway, via Skilak Lake Road.

(10) Skilak Lake outlet into the Kenai River, 2 miles from lower campground.

(11) Bing's Landing, campground and boat launch; parking fee.

(12) Naptowne Rapids (WW3), 10 miles downstream from Skilak Lake and just after Bing's Landing.

(13) Confluence of the Moose and Kenai rivers 3 miles after Naptowne Rapids; Izaak Walton State Campground and boat ramp is about ⅛ mile up the lazy Moose River; land on right bank; highway access is from mile 82 of the Sterling Highway.

(14) Morgan's Landing, campground; parking fee.

(15) Funny River campground.

(16) Swiftwater campground and boat launch; parking fee.

(17) Exit/entrance, Kenai River bridge and Centennial campground at Soldotna, mile 95.9 of the Sterling Highway; parking fee.

(18) Slikok Creek day-use picnic area.

(19) Big Eddy day-use picnic area.

(20) Ciechanski day-use picnic area.

(21) The Pillars boat launch; parking fee.

(22) Tidal action influences river flow beginning halfway between

Upper Kenai River, May

Soldotna and Kenai.

(23) City of Kenai's Cunningham Park, campground and boat launch; highway access is from mile 2.5 of Beaver Loop Road.

(24) Warren Ames bridge and Kenai River Flats day-use picnic area; entrance or exit here is best done at high tide; road access is from Kalifornsky Beach Road.

(25) Kenai boat harbor and boat launch; highway access from the Bridge Access Road between the Kenai Spur Highway and Kalifornsky Beach Road.

Safety dictates that boaters inspect all white water before attempting it. The Schooner Bend rapids can be seen from the access road to the Chugach National Forest Russian River Campground at mile 52.5 of the Sterling Highway. To inspect the Kenai River canyon rapids, drive to mile 58 of the Sterling Highway, and turn south on Skilak Lake Road. Drive 0.7 mile and park at the Kenai River Trail (trip 4) trailhead. Follow an old road 0.2 mile to the Kenai River. The trail then heads uphill to the south and parallels the river downstream. Another access to Kenai River Trail is from mile 2.3 of Skilak Lake Road. When floating the river, double check difficult spots by landing and walking the shoreline to determine the best route around obstacles. The difficulty of rapids will vary according to water level, some becoming more difficult at high water, others less difficult.

Boaters should always wear U.S. Coast Guard–approved flotation vests. Two or more boats should travel together, maintaining sufficient distance between them to allow complete freedom of route. Wear enough warm clothing or, better yet, wet suits, to protect against cold water in case of capsizing. The extreme cold of the water can cause rapid exhaustion and even loss of consciousness. Some of the route is not near a road, and help is often far away.

The Kenai River is extremely popular with anglers and power-boaters as well as nonmotorized boaters. During the July to mid-August red salmon runs, the waters near the confluence with the Russian River are the most intensively fished in the state, with anglers often standing shoulder to shoulder. Avoid tangling with fishing lines as you float by. The river system also produces world-class king salmon weighing up to ninety pounds.

The river is jointly managed by the Alaska Division of Parks and Outdoor Recreation, the U.S. Fish and Wildlife Service, and the U.S. Forest Service (addresses in the Appendix). Motorized used is prohibited year-round from the powerline crossing about a mile below the confluence of the Russian and Kenai rivers to Skilak Lake. From March 15 through June 14, the river is closed to motorized use from the outlet of Skilak Lake downstream for 3 miles.

8 RUSSIAN LAKES– RESURRECTION RIVER TRAIL SYSTEM

LOWER RUSSIAN LAKE
Round trip: 6 miles
Hiking time: 3 hours
High point: 800 feet
Total elevation gain: 300 feet in, 300 feet out
Best: May to October
USGS map: Seward B8

UPPER RUSSIAN LAKE
Round trip: 24 miles
Allow 2 days
High point: 700 feet
Total elevation gain: 800 feet in, 600 feet out
Best: May to October
USGS maps: Seward B8, Kenai B1 NE

Chugach National Forest

COOPER LAKE TO RUSSIAN LAKES
One way: 21.5 miles
Allow 2 days
High point: 1,450 feet
Total elevation gain: 350 feet
Best: June to October
USGS maps: Seward B8, Kenai B1 NE

RUSSIAN LAKES TO RESURRECTION RIVER
One way: 32 miles
Allow 3–5 days
High point: 1,200 feet
Total elevation gain: 1,500 feet
Best: June to October
USGS maps: Seward A7 NW, A8, B8; Kenai B1 NE

The Russian Lakes and Resurrection River trail system offers many possibilities, from an afternoon hike to Lower Russian Lake to a 3–5-day trek nearly to Seward. Combining these options with Resurrection Pass Trail (trip 15) can create a 7–10-day backpacking trip of 70 miles. All options offer beautiful forest walks with cascading clear streams, brilliant wildflowers, berries in season, moose, and bears. Some of the trails offer excellent mountain biking. Glaciated mountains are visible through the trees along most of the trails. Fishing can be excellent in the Russian River, but check fishing regulations before casting.

Russian Lakes

Reach the Russian River Campground trailhead from mile 52.5 of the Sterling Highway (106 miles south of Anchorage). At that point, turn south onto a paved side road marked "Chugach National Forest Campground, Russian River" (do not confuse it with the Kenai National Wildlife Refuge's Kenai–Russian River Campground at mile 55 of the Sterling Highway). Follow the side road to a stop sign and gatehouse. During the salmon runs from mid-June through mid-August, the area is extremely crowded with anglers, and the U.S. Forest Service charges fees for parking, camping, and fishing. Beyond the gatehouse, go left, and follow the road 0.8 mile to a pullout on the left marked for Russian Lakes Trail (elevation 500 feet).

The U.S. Forest Service maintains three cabins along this trail. The Barber cabin is at Lower Russian Lake and comes with a dock and rowboat. The Aspen Flats cabin is 9 miles from the trailhead. A cabin at Upper Russian Lake, 12 miles in, has a boat available for those with reservations. Make reservations with a Forest Service office (addresses in the Appendix).

The hike to Lower Russian Lake (elevation 550 feet) and the Barber cabin is a nice 1-day round trip for families. The trail, of compacted gravel, has been upgraded to difficult wheelchair-accessible standards. After 1.5 miles, the trail comes to a bridge over Rendezvous Creek. At the bridge, there is a fork. The route to Lower Russian Lake crosses the bridge. The other fork avoids the bridge and parallels the creek to just before its confluence with the Russian River.

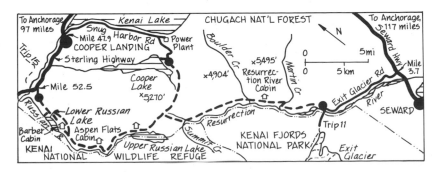

Resurrection River Trail, August (Photo: Helen Nienhueser)

Here the trail forks. The developed trail continues about a quarter mile downstream to the Russian River Cascades and an overlook.

To reach Lower Russian Lake and the Barber cabin, cross Rendezvous Creek and turn right at the *next* fork. To reach Upper Russian Lake (elevation 690 feet), cross Rendezvous Creek, go left at the next fork, and continue south for another 9 miles. The Aspen Flats cabin is between the lakes along a short side trail (marked) that is somewhat more primitive than the main route. In addition, there is an established tent site 40 yards off-trail near a creek in a nice cottonwood forest about halfway to the Aspen Flats cabin.

This trail is not recommended in the winter due to avalanche danger along Lower Russian Lake. The access road is not plowed.

There is a public pay phone near the gatehouse.

Cooper Lake–Russian Lakes

Another fine overnight hike or mountain bike trip is the 21.5-mile trek from Cooper Lake to the Russian River trailhead. The Cooper Lake trailhead (elevation 1,300 feet) is 950 feet higher than the far end—it's downhill most of the way! Check with the Forest Service before setting out, especially on spring trips, to be sure trees blown down across the trail during winter have been cleared. For cyclists wishing to ride a complete loop, there are 17 miles of road riding between the trailheads in addition to the trail riding.

Reach the Cooper Lake trailhead from mile 47.9 of the Sterling Highway (101 miles from Anchorage). Turn southeast on Snug Harbor Road, and follow it a little over 11 miles to a parking area marked by a sign for Russian Lakes trail. The 9-mile trail to Upper Russian Lake is a scenic walk or ride through wooded mountain valleys.

The Cooper Lake to Upper Russian Lake trail makes a good ski trip in winter. It is also used by snowmobiles. Snug Harbor Road is plowed in winter 8.5 miles to the Cooper Lake Power Plant on Kenai Lake. The Russian Lakes end of the trail is prone to avalanches, and the Russian Lakes trailhead access road is not plowed.

Resurrection River Trail

A more strenuous hike, unsuitable for mountain bikes, is to the Resurrection River trailhead (elevation 400 feet) near Seward from either the Russian River trailhead (32 miles) or the Cooper Lake trailhead (21.5 miles). Resurrection River Trail leaves the Upper Russian Lake to Cooper Lake trail about 5.5 miles from the Cooper Lake trailhead and 16 miles from the Russian River trailhead. It descends the Resurrection River drainage for 16 miles. The trail winds through thick forest with occasional glimpses of mountains or the river. The first creek south of Summit Creek has a good campsite, but good camping areas are otherwise scarce. Occasional meadows offer possible tent sites in dry weather. The Forest Service Resurrection River cabin is about 1 mile down the trail south of Boulder Creek, near an unnamed creek.

This trail is managed as a primitive trail from the cabin to the Russian Lakes trail. Boulder Creek (no bridge) can be difficult to cross. Autumn rains can cause flooding, with wading sometimes necessary on the trail. In August and September, the Forest's largest concentration of grizzly bears feeds upstream of the trail crossings for Boulder and Martin creeks. In spring, this stretch of trail often is crossed by hundreds of blown-down trees. The Forest Service removes only the biggest ones. Call to check trail conditions before going.

To reach the Seward end of Resurrection River Trail by road, drive to mile 3.7 of the Seward Highway. Turn onto Exit Glacier Road (marked), and follow it 7.4 miles to a parking area on the right. The trail (also marked) begins about 100 feet farther along the road and parallels the Resurrection River. Much of Resurrection River Trail is poor for skiing.

All the trails are closed to off-road vehicles from May 1 through November 30 and closed to horses from April 1 through June 30. Mountain bikers should observe the spring horse prohibition to avoid eroding soft trails.

9 CRESCENT AND CARTER LAKES

VIA CRESCENT CREEK	VIA CARTER LAKE
Round trip: 13 miles	**Round trip: 6.6 miles**
Hiking time: 5–8 hours	**Hiking time: 3–5 hours**
High point: 1,550 feet	**High point: 1,550 feet**
Total elevation gain: 960 feet in, 100 feet out	**Total elevation gain: 1,050 feet in, 100 feet out**
Best: June to October	**Best: June to October**
USGS maps: Seward B7, C7, C8	**USGS maps: Seward B7, C7**
Traverse: 18.5 miles	

Chugach National Forest

Hike or mountain bike excellent trails to pretty lakes near timberline. Either the Crescent Creek Trail or the Carter Lake Trail makes a glorious September hike through the golds and reds of autumn. The trip is good for families with children if they have reservations for overnight use of the U.S. Forest Service cabin located at the west end of Crescent Lake. A rowboat goes with the cabin, and fishing for grayling is good. The east end of Crescent Lake is accessible via the shorter but steeper Carter Lake Trail. Unless the cabin is the main objective, the east end of the lake is a nice alternate trip. Nine miles of more primitive trail, unsuitable for bikes, connect the two ends of the lake along its south side. Another cabin, the Crescent Saddle Cabin, lies about halfway along this connector trail.

Camping is good near both ends of the lake, although the western end has been so popular that the Forest Service has recently disallowed camping in some overworn spots until vegetation grows back. Please be aware of your impact on the land, and try to avoid further damage. The only campsites on the traverse are in the middle, between a creek coming from a low pass and some islands in the lake. Water is available, but the wood supply is primarily brush. Moose and bears may be spotted in summer, wolverine occasionally in winter. The two main trails are described in more detail below.

Crescent Creek Trail

To reach the Crescent Lake trailhead, drive to mile 44.9 of the Sterling Highway, 98 miles south of Anchorage, and turn south on a road marked "Quartz Creek Recreation Area." Follow this road 3.3 miles to the start of Crescent Creek Trail (marked), 0.5 mile beyond Crescent Creek Campground.

Crescent Creek Trail starts directly across the road from the parking area (elevation 590 feet). The path winds gently through birch and aspen woods along a tiny stream, climbs over a low ridge, and descends into Crescent Creek canyon. Follow the trail upstream, crossing the creek on a bridge, and continue upward, often on the hillside well above the creek. The trail wanders through patches of woods and across avalanche-cleared swaths, finally emerging in a broad, open meadow dotted with trees. Cross Crescent Creek again, on a bridge near the lake outlet (elevation 1,454 feet). The cabin is a short distance

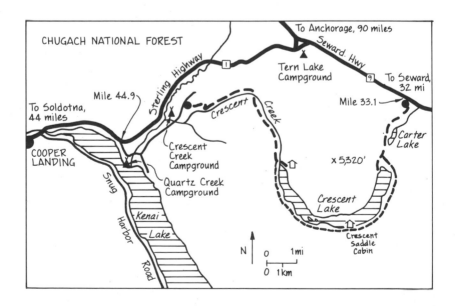

61

Crescent Creek at Crescent Lake, September

along the lakeshore beyond the bridge. Make cabin reservations through a Forest Service office (addresses in the Appendix). High country is accessible from here.

Crescent Creek Trail is hazardous in winter due to avalanches (see "Avalanches" in the Introduction), and even in spring, the deep, dense snow in avalanche paths melts last, leaving slippery footing on this route that is otherwise known for its fine, broad trail.

Carter Lake Trail

To reach Crescent Lake via Carter Lake, drive to mile 33.1 of the Seward Highway (94 miles south of Anchorage). The trail leaves from a parking area on the west side of the highway (elevation 500 feet). Cross a footbridge at the trailhead, and climb the switchbacks of this pleasant but steep 2.3-mile trail to Carter Lake (elevation 1,486 feet). A smaller trail continues another mile around the west side of the lake and on to Crescent Lake. The trail forks a third of a mile before Crescent Lake. The left fork, marked by a large rock cairn, leads around Crescent Lake. In winter, Carter Lake Trail makes an excellent ski tour; skiers can continue across Crescent Lake to the cabins.

All these trails are closed to vehicles from May 1 through November 30. They are closed to horses from April 1 through June 30 because of soft trail conditions. Mountain bikers should observe the horse prohibitions to help avoid causing trail erosion.

10 MOUNT MARATHON, RACE POINT

Round trip: 3–4 miles
Hiking time: 43 minutes to 7 hours
High point: 3,022 feet

Total elevation gain: 2,900 feet
Best: April to October
USGS map: Seward A7 SW

City of Seward and Alaska Division of Land

In 1915, the year completion of a railroad from Seward led to the founding of Anchorage, a bet in Seward started a race still repeated every 4th of July. The runners in this mountain marathon start from the town center near sea level, climb to Race Point (elevation 3,022 feet) at the end of the southeast ridge of Marathon Mountain, and return. The record is 43 minutes, 11 seconds, set in 1981 by Bill Spencer. Independence Day is the most exciting time to make the climb, whether you are in the race or not, but it is a good hike anytime during the summer.

A hikers' trail and the runners' trail climb toward Race Point, although the hikers' trail has an easier destination as well. The hikers' trail is steep—the runners' trail is even steeper. Fortunately, each provides a spectacular view of Seward and Resurrection Bay, giving ready excuse for pause. You may choose to go up the hikers' trail and down the runners' trail; the two lower ends are within easy walking distance.

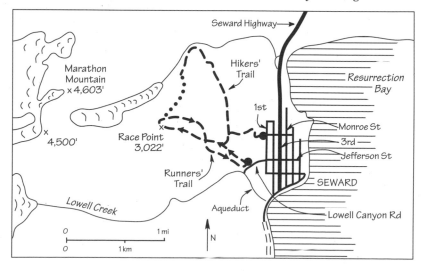

The Runners' Trail

To reach the well-known runners' trail, find Jefferson Street in Seward, and drive on it toward the base of Marathon Mountain. At First Avenue, it becomes Lowell Canyon Road, which soon ends at the Lowell Creek Picnic Area and a gate. Park on the left (elevation 200 feet). The trail begins behind the picnic tables and leads around the back of the large water tanks. The race route follows the road beyond the gate, veering slightly to the right. Both trail and road lead quickly to the base of the mountain proper and a sign that reads "Mt. Marathon Race Trail."

Duck into the woods at the sign, and start uphill. The first section of the trail is steepest—a forested cliff requiring the use of handholds. Test holds before depending on them, and be careful not to knock debris on other hikers below. The hands and feet of runners have worn several paths up this initial section. Pick the route that looks best, but do stay in the trees and avoid the rock outcrops and gully farther to the left. If all of this looks intimidating, consider backtracking to the hikers' trail instead.

For those who continue, the angle eases from cliff to merely steep, and the several trails merge into one. The trail follows a ridge crest above and to the right of the gully. The runners' trail has separate up and down routes that form a figure eight. Emerging from the trees, the ascent route continues up the ridge and is crossed by the down route, which enters from the right and descends into the gully on the left. Unless you are a runner, sit a while to enjoy the impressive view of Resurrection Bay and the glacier-streaked mountains beyond. Look for ptarmigan, ground squirrels, marmots, mountain goats, Dall sheep, and a wide variety of wildflowers.

The trail to the "summit" at 3,022 feet becomes poorly defined on the rocky ridge; just continue toward the skyline. Race Point is the nearly level ridge top that appears suddenly. The descent route starts down the east face of the mountain. Snow patches remain near the top well into July. Although runners slide on the snow for a quick descent, hikers should note that this is where many runners injure themselves. The snow is steep and fast and ends in rock. It is easy enough to avoid the snow, and below, descending with long strides in loose gravel (scree) is fun. Descending in the gully in the first half of summer often involves crossing snow. The gully ends in cliffs. Although many runners descend the cliffs, most hikers will want to exit the gully and return to the route they ascended through the trees. Just above the cliffs, look for a trail to the left. It rejoins the ascent route.

The Hikers' Trail

Reach the hikers' trail by following First Avenue along the base of Marathon Mountain to its intersection with Munroe Street. Between two houses, a yellow gate blocks vehicle access to an old track up the hillside. Park at the gate (elevation 200 feet), and start immediately uphill. Round two switchbacks, and relax on an easier grade as you reach a fork. Go left; the right fork dead-ends. Within 5 minutes, go right at another fork. Within a few more minutes, the wide main trail passes a large hemlock with an orange arrow spray-painted on its bark. Follow the narrow trail indicated by the arrow to join the runners' trail (and be sure to note this intersection if you wish to return the same way, as it could be hard to find on the way down). Ignore the arrow, and stay on the main trail for a different adventure.

The main trail appears to end a short time later at a small, fenced reservoir and dam near treeline. Walk along the fence uphill of the reservoir and find a well-defined but much narrower footpath that parallels a creek. If it seems odd that this creek runs across the face of Marathon Mountain instead of directly down the face, it is because it is a channel hand-dug in the early 1900s to bring drinking water to Seward. The mostly gentle grade leads eventually to a ridge that drops toward the northeast off Race Point. Round this ridge, and step into a beautiful alpine cirque beneath the true summit of Marathon Mountain. The northeast ridge is a longer but less-steep alternate for ascending to Race Point, but most hikers venturing this way will be satisfied with making the cirque their destination. Just as the trail enters the cirque, listen for a waterfall, and make your way north to see it. Snow can obscure the upper end of this trail well into the summer.

To climb the true summit of Marathon Mountain (elevation 4,750 feet) by any route requires experience and mountaineering gear.

Resurrection Bay from hikers' trail, August (Photo: John Wolfe Jr.)

11 EXIT GLACIER AND HARDING ICEFIELD

Round trip: up to 7.5 miles
Hiking time: 4–8 hours
High point: 3,400 feet

Total elevation gain: 3,000 feet
Best: June to September
USGS maps: Seward A7 NW, A8

Kenai Fjords National Park

While valley glaciers typically nestle between high peaks, icefields bury mountains entirely or leave just their tops—called *nunataks*—jutting out of the ice. Harding Icefield Trail may be the only established trail in the country that leads to an icefield overlook. Getting there is a stiff uphill walk, but the trail parallels the frozen blue-white waterfall that is Exit Glacier all the way. Views of the glacier contrast sharply with the deep green of thick summer foliage and the magenta of fireweed blooms to create a memorable walk even for those who tire before reaching the highest point.

To reach the trailhead at the toe of Exit Glacier, drive to mile 3.7 of the Seward Highway, on the edge of the city of Seward, and turn west on Exit Glacier Road (marked). Proceed 8.9 miles on this gravel road to a parking area (elevation 400 feet) a short distance from a National Park Service ranger station. A paved, wheelchair-accessible path (bikes are not allowed) leads toward the ranger station and the obvious

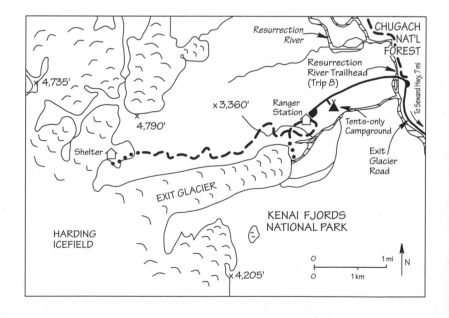

Exit Glacier, August (Photo: John Wolfe Jr.)

hunk of ice spilling off the mountainsides. After a quarter of a mile, the paved trail ends near a shelter kiosk. A short distance farther, a "Harding Icefield Trail" sign directs hikers to the right. The less ambitious will enjoy a network of short trails around the toe of the glacier, including a loop back to the ranger station.

On Harding Icefield Trail, hikers will appreciate the work of the Student Conservation Association. High school students have worked for several summers to carve a beautiful trail with relatively easy grades from the steep hillside, but a small rock outcrop within 20 minutes of the sign is an exception. Those who feel uncomfortable crossing the rock probably will not be comfortable with some of the upper parts of the trail either. On the other hand, it is the only part of the trail for a couple of miles that is not a prepared path. Beyond the outcrop, the view of the glacier through the trees and from frequent overlooks steadily improves.

Eventually, above treeline, the trail becomes less distinct. Early in the season, steps in leftover snow will usually guide hikers. Later in the summer, if the trail seems to peter out as you crest a rise and get your first view of the icefield, aim toward a black-rock cliff that faces Exit Glacier. Before reaching the cliff, turn right and head up the right-hand side of a creek to a low saddle, crossing the creek just below the saddle crest. From there, the route is relatively straightforward. It is little more than half an hour from that spot to the high point overlooking the icefield and its many nunataks.

Hikers should prepare at any time of year for ice-cold winds that often blow off the Harding Icefield, even on sunny days. Bad weather can roll in quickly in this area, too, and because of this, the Park Service has established an emergency mountain shelter near the icefield. It is on a hill of gravel and rock on the route, but it does not overlook the icefield. It cannot be reserved but may be used by anybody in bad weather. Limited camping is possible in this area.

Wherever this route is above treeline, hikers should stay on the main trail and observe any park signs about trail use. Old scars evident on the tundra should be ample reminder that even walkers can impact the land. Those camping should set up only at the top end of the trail on bare rock and gravel or on snow to avoid damaging the fragile alpine plants that may take more than a century to regenerate.

Only experienced mountaineers with crevasse rescue training and proper equipment should venture onto the icefield. Some other notes: (1) a small tents-only campground near the trailhead parking lot offers the only free camping in the Seward area; (2) Exit Glacier Road is not maintained in winter, from November 1 to May 1, but the Resurrection River valley offers some fine ski touring when snow conditions are good, and Park Service buildings are available near the Exit Glacier trailhead for public use in the winter; and (3) the park's headquarters, which can provide more information, is in Seward, just south of the harbormaster's building and adjacent to the small boat harbor.

12   LOST LAKE

Round trip: 14 miles
Traverse: 15 miles
Hiking time: 7–10 hours
High point: 2,000 feet
Best: July to September

Total elevation gain: from Primrose
   Landing 1,600 feet; from
   southern trailhead 1,900 feet
USGS maps: Seward A7 NE, B7 SE

Chugach National Forest

In July this is perhaps the most beautiful and photogenic trail the Kenai Peninsula has to offer. Climbing through a hemlock and spruce forest, the trail emerges above treeline on tundra and flowered meadows accented by stands of weathered, gnarled hemlocks. The area was at one time heavily glaciated; now brilliant blue lakes fill every depression, reflecting the snow-covered summits of surrounding mountains. Lost Lake, the largest, is forced into a strange shape by the topography. The area invites camping and exploring. Water is plentiful but firewood scarce, so take a cooking stove. A few small fish populate Lost Lake, and marmots abound in the nearby rock slides. The trail is good for family outings and ski or snowshoe trips.

This trail has two trailheads. The northern trailhead is in Primrose Campground on Kenai Lake and the southern trailhead is in Lost Lake Subdivision, mile 5.3 of the Seward Highway.

To reach the Primrose trailhead, turn off the Seward Highway at mile 17.1 at a sign for Primrose Landing Campground (110 miles south of Anchorage). Drive about a mile to the end of the access road, and park in the boat ramp area at the entrance to the campground. The trailhead (elevation 450 feet) is about 1,000 feet back from the lake at the end of the campground road and is well marked. The generally excellent trail climbs gradually for about 5 miles through spruce and hemlock forest to timberline and then crosses about 2 miles of meadows and ridge tops to reach Lost Lake (elevation 1,920 feet). Take time for a short side trip on an unmarked route through the woods to a pretty waterfall a little over 2 miles up the trail from the campground. If the clouds close in above timberline, follow the wooden 4x4 markers to the lake. In some years snow may persist into July, making the trail above timberline hard to follow. If snow or fog obscure the trail, note where it emerges onto the ridge so that you can find it on your return. A white wooden diamond high on a tree may mark the trail.

To reach the southern trailhead, drive to mile 5.3 of the Seward Highway (122 miles south of Anchorage). Turn west into Lost Lake Subdivision, and follow the road uphill 0.2 mile to a T intersection. Turn left on Heather Lee Lane and go straight for 0.2 mile to an intersection; turn right and drive 0.3 mile to the end of the road and the trailhead (elevation 400 feet). The trail takes off to the left (northwest) near the end of the road.

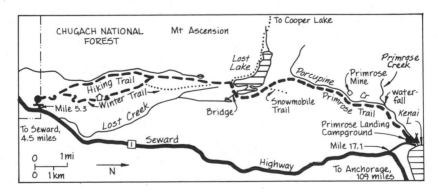

The trail climbs gently through coniferous forest. There are several forks in the first mile of the trail. The first right-hand fork is an alternate route around a steep section of the trail. It rejoins the main trail at the second intersection. The third intersection is a winter trail that branches off to the right. Follow the left-hand trail, which winds through a pleasant forested canyon. Salmonberries are ripe in August along the trail near mile 4. Resurrection Bay occasionally can be seen glistening in the distance. The latter part of the route is entirely above brushline. At about mile 6, the trail emerges on a glacier-scarred bedrock bench and, in another mile, reaches Lost Lake.

A traverse is a delightful way to do this trip, which can be started from either end. Starting at Primrose Campground cuts the elevation gain by 300 feet and offers views of Resurrection Bay ahead of you on the descent to the southern trailhead. There is a bridge across Lost Creek, the outlet of Lost Lake, at about mile 7½. The bridge is generally snow-free from mid-June into early September.

Climbing to the summit of Mount Ascension (elevation 5,710 feet), the prominent peak west of Lost Lake, is a goal best left to mountaineers, who will need ice axes and crampons. However, scrambling part way up the steep lower slopes for a sweeping view is definitely recom-

Camp at Lost Lake, July

mended. A side trip, easy walking over firm tundra, around the southwest edge of the lake and up the valley to the west brings a splendid view of the steep north side of Mount Ascension. Look for mountain goats and bears. A cross-country hike from here to Cooper Lake is possible (see trip 8).

The Dale Clemens Memorial Forest Service cabin is located on a spur trail about 1½ miles off the main Lost Lake trail; the intersection is about 4 miles from the southern trailhead and a little over 11 miles from the northern trailhead. This beautiful little cabin has room for as many as ten people to sleep. The cabin offers sweeping views of Resurrection Bay and Seward as well as nearby Resurrection Peaks. In winter the cabin is accessible from the southern trailhead via the winter trail. Contact the Forest Service to rent the cabin (address in the Appendix).

The winter trail is popular with snowmobilers. Parts of the winter trail can be icy, fairly steep, and marginal for skiing, although there can be excellent springtime skiing in the vicinity of the cabin. Skiers may want to walk the first part of the trail.

The entire area is open to mining, and there are several active claims in the vicinity of Primrose Trail. At least one miner has a permit to use an all-terrain vehicle on Primrose Trail to reach his claim.

The Forest Service does not recommend the use of mountain bikes on Primrose Trail. The south end of Lost Lake Trail is rated as moderately difficult to difficult for mountain bikes. Stay on the trail, and do not take bikes north of the bridge to avoid damaging the fragile alpine terrain. The trail is closed to motorized vehicles from May 1 through November 30 (except miners under permit) and closed to horses from April 1 through June 30. Mountain bikers should observe the horse-prohibition period to avoid trail erosion when the trails are soft.

13 PTARMIGAN LAKE

Round trip: 7–15 miles
Hiking time: 3–8 hours
High point: 900 feet
Best: May to October

Total elevation gain: 450 feet in,
150 feet out
USGS maps: Seward B6, B7

Chugach National Forest

A turquoise beauty, Ptarmigan Lake reflects the mountains that surround it. Two trails with magnificent views lead from the highway to join shortly before the lake; a 4-mile extension of the trail continues around the lake to its east end.

Entering by one trailhead and leaving by the other makes a nice loop trip; the trailheads are only a mile apart. High grasses may obscure the turnoff to the northern trail when you return from Ptarmigan Lake, so the loop is best hiked beginning at the northern trailhead.

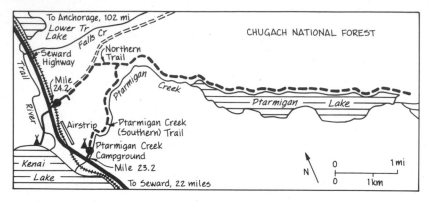

Anglers will find grayling, salmon, Dolly Varden, and rainbow trout in Ptarmigan Creek and grayling in Ptarmigan Lake.

To reach the northern trailhead, drive to mile 24.2 of the Seward Highway (103 miles south of Anchorage). Just north of the Trail River Campground entrance, and on the opposite side of the highway, turn onto a gravel road with a stop sign and yellow mailbox. Proceed east across a set of railroad tracks, and park near the tracks (elevation 450 feet).

On foot, continue east a short distance. The road passes a house and an old log cabin. Respect private property. Near the old cabin, the main road turns right to another house. Instead of turning right, pass around a Forest Service gate straight ahead, and start up the trail. A sign may mark the trailhead: "Falls Creek 3; Ptarmigan Lake Access Trail 1." The trail is not well maintained, however, so signs may be down. Ptarmigan Lake is about 3 miles away. The first mile follows an old mining road.

Just uphill beyond a creek crossing and the remains of a burned cabin in a clearing, the trail turns right, leaving the old road. The trail climbs a low timbered ridge and then contours along the mountainside at about 900 feet elevation, well above the valley floor. Look for glimpses of Ptarmigan and Kenai lakes. Soon this trail intersects Ptarmigan Creek Trail, which originates at Ptarmigan Creek Campground. Continue straight ahead to Ptarmigan Lake (elevation 755 feet).

This can be destination enough for a picnic or overnight camping, or continue around the north shore of the lake about 4 miles to the eastern end, which also offers good campsites.

The southern trailhead, for Ptarmigan Creek Trail, leaves from Ptarmigan Creek Campground (elevation 450 feet) at mile 23.2 of the Seward Highway. The scenic trail, 3½ miles long, follows the tumbling clear creek upstream and then turns away to climb through a quiet conifer forest to meet the northern trail.

The route originally continued beyond Ptarmigan Lake into Paradise Valley. It is now badly overgrown, but those with an exploring bent might want to tackle the old path.

Avalanche hazard precludes winter use of either trail beyond the first 1½ miles. Hikers traveling via light planes can land on the

Ptarmigan Lake, July (Photo: Gayle Nienhueser)

Lawing airstrip between the trailheads. Ptarmigan Creek Trail is closed to horses from April 1 through June 30 and to motorized vehicles May 1 through November 30. Mountain bikers may use the northern trailhead and follow the mining road 3 miles to Falls Creek, although the route is not easy. The routes to Ptarmigan Lake are not suitable for bikes.

14 JOHNSON PASS

Traverse: 23 miles
Allow 2 days hiking, 1 day mountain biking
High point: 1,450 feet
Total elevation gain: 700 feet southbound, 1,000 feet northbound
Best: June to September
USGS maps: Seward C6, C7

Chugach National Forest

Between 1908 and 1910, the Alaska Road Commission constructed a trail for pack horses and dog teams through Johnson Pass en route to the gold fields of the Iditarod area. The first shipment of gold, over a half million dollars worth, left Iditarod in December 1911 and took 54 days to reach Seward. This hiking and mountain biking trail follows portions of that route; watch for traces of the old trail.

To reach the Granite Creek (northern) trailhead just south of Turnagain Pass, drive to mile 63.8 of the Seward Highway (63 miles south of Anchorage). A 0.4-mile side road, marked Johnson Pass, leads south to a parking area (elevation 750 feet). The southern trailhead (elevation 450 feet) is at mile 32.7 of the Seward Highway, near Upper Trail Lake and its fish hatchery.

From the Granite Creek trailhead, the route winds through open meadows and forest, crossing Center Creek (mile 2.2) and Bench Creek (mile 3.8) on bridges. Walking only as far as either bridge makes a pleasant day's outing. Beyond the second bridge, the trail enters V-shaped Bench Creek valley and follows the creek to its source at Ohio Creek and Bench Lake. Cyclists, especially, will note a couple of short, steep stretches with some loose gravel.

After crossing Ohio Creek (mile 8.9), the trail follows the eastern shore of Bench Lake and climbs imperceptibly to Johnson Pass (mile 10; elevation 1,450 feet). South of Johnson Lake, the trail parallels Johnson Creek but is above the creek in the woods. About 9 miles south of the pass, the trail emerges on the shore of Upper Trail Lake and follows the shore to the southern trailhead.

Good campsites can be found at Johnson Pass above timberline and at the south end of Johnson Lake (mile 11). Careless campers have left toilet paper and feces near the lakeshore in at least one spot. Be sure to bury feces at least 200 feet from any surface water, and carry toilet paper out with you.

The Center Creek valley and the first 7 miles of trail from the southern trailhead make good ski trips, but stay well away from slopes that could avalanche (see "Avalanches" in the Introduction). Winter travel through the pass between the Bench Creek bridge and mile 12, 2 miles south of Johnson Lake, is not recommended due to severe avalanche hazard.

The trail from the Bench Creek bridge to the northern trailhead and all of the Center Creek drainage are closed to motorized vehicles year-

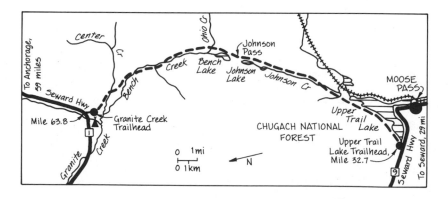

Johnson Lake, July

round; other parts of the trail are closed to them from May 1 through November 30. The trail is closed to horses from April 1 through June 30 because of soft trail conditions. Mountain bikers should observe this prohibition to avoid causing trail erosion.

15 RESURRECTION PASS TRAIL SYSTEM

Traverse: up to 38.6 miles
Allow 3–6 days hiking, 2 days mountain biking
High point: 2,600 feet
Best: June to September

Chugach National Forest

Total elevation gain: 2,100 feet southbound, 2,200 feet northbound
USGS maps: Seward B8, C7, C8, D8

Hikers or mountain bikers looking for a long trip, a good trail, mountain scenery, cabins, and fishing all at once will find them along the

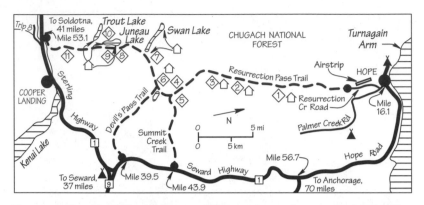

Resurrection Pass Trail system. The most popular route, 38.6 miles between the Hope trailhead and the Sterling Highway, normally takes 3 days for strong hikers in good condition and 5 or more for families. Strong cyclists ride it in a day, but it is one of few single track trails that make good 2- or even 3-day rides. This route was traveled in the late 1890s by gold seekers coming from Resurrection Bay to the gold fields near Hope. Today it is a designated National Recreation Trail.

To begin the trail at the Hope trailhead, drive to mile 56.7 of the Seward Highway (71 miles south of Anchorage). Turn north onto Hope Road, drive to mile 16.1, and then turn left onto Resurrection Creek Road. Be alert for a right-angle turn (marked), and turn right at it. Drive a total of 4 miles from Hope Road to the trailhead (elevation 500 feet) at Resurrection Creek. The trail begins by crossing the creek on a bridge.

The cabins are well spaced for a 5-day hike, although families may prefer a longer trip using more cabins. Make cabin reservations with a U.S. Forest Service office (addresses in the Appendix) well in advance. For those not using the cabins, campsites are easy to find.

The trail follows the wooded Resurrection Creek valley and quickly narrows to a well-maintained path that occasionally climbs in and out of side-stream drainages. Above treeline near the creek's headwaters, the trail is a narrow ribbon buried deep in wildflowers. Watch for moose, Dall sheep, marmots, and grizzly (brown) bears. Resurrection Pass itself is covered in low alpine tundra; there is no firewood. The trail descends the Juneau Creek valley through forests and beside mountain lakes to the Sterling Highway.

Three other trails connect with this main route to make an intriguing trail system: Devil's Pass Trail to the Seward Highway; Summit Creek Trail to the Seward Highway; and the Russian Lakes–Resurrection River trail system, on the south side of the Sterling Highway, which leads almost to Seward. Hikes from the Hope trailhead to either of the Seward Highway trailheads are about 31 miles. From either of the Seward Highway trailheads to the Sterling Highway is about 27 miles. From one Seward Highway trailhead to the other is about 20 miles. A trek across the Sterling Highway and on to Exit Glacier Road (see trip

8) can total 70 miles. On the Resurrection Pass system, only the main route is recommended for mountain bikes.

Points of interest, keyed to the map and measured from the Hope trailhead, are the following:

(1) Caribou Creek cabin at mile 7.1.
(2) Fox Creek cabin at mile 12.5.
(3) East Creek cabin at mile 14.4.
(4) Resurrection Pass, elevation 2,600 feet, at mile 19.3.
(5) Summit Creek Trail access at the pass.
(6) Devil's Pass cabin and Devil's Pass Trail junction at mile 21.4.
(7) Swan Lake cabin at mile 25.8, and a bushwhacking route to West Swan Lake cabin.
(8) Juneau Lake cabin site at mile 29.1 (cabin burned in 1997; it may be rebuilt).
(9) Romig cabin on Juneau Lake at mile 30.
(10) Trout Lake cabin via a half-mile side trail at mile 31.8.
(11) Juneau Creek falls at mile 34.1.

Former Juneau Lake cabin, July 1990 (Photo: Helen Nienhueser)

The lake cabins all have boats available for cabin renters, and there are fish in the lakes. The trail terminates a few dozen yards off the Sterling Highway at mile 53.1 (elevation 450 feet), just west of the Kenai River near Schooner Bend.

Devil's Pass Trail begins at John's Creek, at mile 39.5 of the Seward Highway (elevation 1,000 feet), and climbs to 2,400-foot Devil's Pass. It joins Resurrection Pass Trail at about the same elevation. This is an easy trail with a gradual elevation gain.

To locate the Summit Creek trailhead, turn west off the Seward Highway at mile 43.9. Hidden behind the trees is a parking area and, at the south end, a trailhead bulletin board (elevation 1,350 feet). There is no sign for the trail on the highway. The trail climbs uphill and then traverses above and north of Summit Creek. Nearly two miles in, it joins the original route, which followed the creek. The route crosses two passes (elevations 3,450 and 3,350 feet) and descends to Resurrection Pass. Finding Summit Creek Trail from Resurrection Pass Trail can be difficult.

The main route from Hope to the Sterling Highway makes a fine ski or snowshoe tour in winter, but prepare for blizzards in the pass and, in midwinter, the possibility of below-zero temperatures. Devil's Pass and Summit Creek trails are not recommended due to severe avalanche hazard (see "Avalanches" in the Introduction).

Resurrection Pass and Devil's Pass trails are closed to vehicles, including snowmobiles, from February 16 through November 30 and closed to horses from April 1 through June 30 because of soft spring trail conditions. Mountain bikers should observe the horse prohibition as well to help prevent trail erosion.

16 PALMER CREEK LAKES

Round trip: 2 miles or more
Hiking time: 1–4 hours
High point: 2,950 feet or more
Best: July to September

Total elevation gain: 750 feet
or more
USGS map: Seward D7

Chugach National Forest

High in the hills above the old mining community of Hope is the scenic valley of Palmer Creek. Here, the tundra is punctuated by waterfalls and weathered hemlocks. Higher yet, a hanging valley cradles two alpine lakes. This is a delightful day trip for children and agile grandparents alike. The only sobering note is the last 5 miles of road—high, narrow, winding—but normally driveable in dry weather by most cars with sufficiently high clearance. The road is unsafe for large camper vehicles and trailers but is good for mountain bikes.

Ridge walking, July.

Gold was first discovered along Palmer Creek by George Palmer in 1894. A rush to the Turnagain goldfields took place in 1896. Two towns, Hope and Sunrise, grew out of the rush, and as many as 5,000 people were reported living in the area in 1898. Palmer Creek was the site of early placer mining and, later, lode mining, beginning in 1911

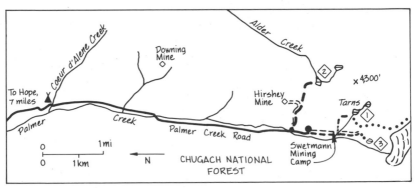

Tarn above Palmer Creek, July (Photo: Helen Nienhueser)

with John Hirshey's Lucky Strike vein. Mining continued into the 1930s, and several claims in the area are active today.

At mile 56.7 of the Seward Highway (71 miles south of Anchorage), turn north at Hope Road, drive about 16 miles, then turn left onto Resurrection Creek Road. In 0.7 mile, continue straight on Palmer Creek Road, following it about 11.4 miles to a gate marked "Lucky Strike Mine." A Forest Service gate at a bridge 0.3 mile before may be closed. A driver may choose to stop even sooner to protect his car's finish from brush or to avoid fording areas flooded by beaver activity. The road is not maintained beyond the Coeur d'Alene Campground at mile 7.

On foot, follow the road beyond the gate about a half mile to a stream flowing from the east. This is the area marked as "Swetman Camp" on topographic maps. The trail begins about 30 feet before the stream (elevation 2,200 feet). It climbs the hillside to the east and leads to a pretty hanging valley (1) with tarns (alpine lakes). Although steep, the trail is less than a mile long. It passes a waterfall. Reach a larger waterfall by cutting south across the hillside below the steepest part of the trail—a nice detour on the way down. The tarns, nestled at 2,950 feet below sheer rock walls, are fine picnic spots.

Hikers who enjoy rock scrambling will find many inviting ridges and small peaks in the area. A ridge particularly easy to climb is southwest of the tarns, between the tarns and the main Palmer Creek valley. It is an easy hour's walk up this ridge to a view of the small glacier at the head of Palmer Creek valley. This glacier, not shown on the topographic map, is the remnant of the glacier that carved the Palmer Creek valley. Snow lingers on the ridges until well into July.

Another set of lakes (2) lies at about 3,000 feet elevation at the head of Alder Creek, just over the ridge above the Hirshey mine. Use the road to the Hirshey mine to reach these lakes; it turns off the main road at the Forest Service gate. Some of the Kenai Peninsula's elusive caribou may be spotted on upper Alder Creek. Finally, try following Palmer Creek Road up the valley about another mile toward a small knob with a fine view. A tiny gemlike tarn (3) lies hidden behind the knob.

Camp at Coeur d'Alene Campground or well away from the trails and lakes to minimize impact on the fragile tundra. Children will enjoy fishing for golden fin trout in the beaver ponds along Palmer Creek.

The mining buildings are private property and should be left alone. Elevation and northern exposure often keep the road in this valley closed until July. Avalanche danger makes this area hazardous in winter and spring.

17 HOPE POINT

Round trip: 5 miles
Hiking time: 4–8 hours
High point: 3,706 feet

Total elevation gain: 3,600 feet
Best: May to October
USGS map: Seward D8

Chugach National Forest

Spectacular, though very steep, the route to Hope Point offers impressive views of Turnagain Arm from a different angle than is usually available. The vista north across Turnagain Arm puts into perspective those familiar Chugach Mountains southeast of Anchorage. Take extra maps (Seward B7, and Anchorage A7 and A8) to help locate favorite spots.

At mile 56.7 of the Seward Highway (71 miles south of Anchorage), turn north onto the scenic 18-mile Hope Road. Drive past Hope, continuing another mile to the road's end at Chugach National Forest Porcupine Campground. Park in the campground at the parking lot for the Gull Rock trailhead (trip 18; elevation 100 feet).

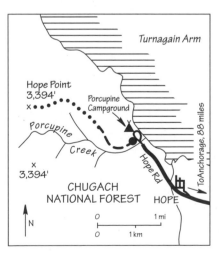

Walk the campground road back toward the entrance as far as Porcupine Creek. A marked, minimally maintained foot trail follows the right-hand side of the stream and makes a lovely creekside walk beside water tumbling gently over mossy rocks. This meandering trail under a forest canopy lasts ⅓ mile.

Turnagain Arm from ridge below Hope Point, October

The trail then climbs the bluff to the right and continues steeply upward through forest. Soon the trees thin, and hikers enter an inclined meadow parkland studded with evergreens. Climb at least to the beginning of this area at the first rocky outcropping (800 feet), far enough to get a view up the Resurrection Creek valley. The valley is particularly pretty in autumn when the birch and aspen forest is a brilliant gold. Plan on taking about 15 minutes to stroll along the stream and another half hour to reach the outcropping. To this point the trip is suitable for children with some experience. At the outcropping you are nearly at timberline. The trail continues upward very steeply for perhaps another half hour. Then the angle eases, and the route all the way to Hope Point (elevation 3,706 feet) is laid out ahead. The route passes a radio repeater, perched on the ridge crest. Follow this ridge crest to the top.

En route are sweeping views of Turnagain Arm, the mountains rimming it, Cook Inlet, and Fire Island. Watch for a bore tide, the well-defined leading wave of an incoming tide. Grass and moss with scrub hemlock and a few alder patches, crowberries, bearberries, caribou lichen, and ground cedar cover the slopes. Moose and bear droppings are abundant, so watch for the animals themselves.

On the steepest stretches, trail erosion could become a problem. Hikers should try to stay on the trail and not contribute to making the eroded section wider by trampling the fragile tundra plants alongside.

From Hope Point the ridge to the south beckons for miles. Lack of water is the most limiting factor (expect no water after Porcupine Creek), although in early summer snow patches should be available for melting. Plan to spend as much time as possible in this alpine wonderland.

18 GULL ROCK

Round trip: 10.2 miles
Hiking time: 4–7 hours
High point: 650 feet
Best: May to October

Total elevation gain: 550 feet in,
510 feet out
USGS map: Seward D8

Chugach National Forest and Kenai National Wildlife Refuge

To enjoy an easy trail with views of the ocean, take this delightful path to Gull Rock along the southwest side of Turnagain Arm. Watch for moose on the land, beluga whales in the water, and bald eagles in the air. The views of the Arm and the mountains beyond are especially nice in spring and fall when the trees bordering the trail are free of leaves. Hikers and mountain bikers of any age will appreciate this gentle trail.

An old wagon road built in the late 1920s, the trail leaves the Hope area and parallels Turnagain Arm west for 5.1 miles. Although today's trail ends at Gull Rock, the wagon road—no longer maintained or free of brush—connects with a tractor trail a few miles to the west where a natural gas pipeline from the Swanson River oil field crosses

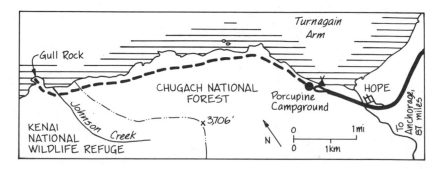

Turnagain Arm. The reminders of earlier days are fascinating: the remains of a cabin and stable on Johnson Creek near the end of the trail, a mossy old bridge that once crossed the creek, and the ruins of a sawmill.

To reach the trailhead, drive to mile 56.7 of the Seward Highway (71 miles south of Anchorage). Turn north onto 18-mile Hope Road and drive around Hope, continuing another mile to the road's end at Porcupine Campground. The trailhead (elevation 100 feet) is at the far end of the campground.

Winding along the shoreline well above tidewater, the trail reaches an elevation of 650 feet at one point before it drops back down to Gull Rock. The way is never steep, and walking is pleasant, although mountain bikers will find a few slippery spots and a lot of bumpy roots. Breaks in the trees afford views of the Arm and shoreline. The variety of vegetation along the trail is interesting: from pleasant birch and

Turnagain Arm from Gull Rock, November

aspen woods to alder-choked gullies, from stately hemlock forests carpeted by deep moss to a tundra-like area with tiny spruce, mosses, lichens, lingonberries, and saxifrages. At one point the trail crosses an avalanche gully so steep and straight that it looks like a suicidal bobsled run that ends in Turnagain Arm.

Beyond Johnson Creek, continue on the trail to the rocky promontory of Gull Rock (elevation 140 feet). It is near Johnson Creek that the trail enters the Kenai National Wildlife Refuge; mountain bikes are not allowed beyond the Refuge boundary marker, but Gull Rock is just a short walk farther. At the trail's end, sit and listen to the turbulent water swirl around the rocks below as the tides flow in and out. On the other side of Turnagain Arm, a tiny stream of cars flows by on the Seward Highway near McHugh Creek Picnic Area.

Water can be found along the trail, but the only reasonable tent sites are at Gull Rock, where fresh water is not immediately at hand and where, unfortunately, some campers have impacted the area for all. Some trees have been denuded for firewood, and there are multiple old fire pits. This is best treated as a day hike, but those who do camp should bring a gas stove and avoid building a fire. The best camping is at Porcupine Campground.

The trail is closed to motorized vehicles from May 1 through November 30 and to horses from April 1 through June 30. Mountain bikers should observe the horse prohibition to avoid causing trail erosion when the trail is soft. Also, cyclists should recognize that the route is popular with walkers of all ages and should not take the trail's easy grades as invitation to ride so fast as to surprise them.

19 TURNAGAIN PASS SKI TOUR

Round trip: 6 miles
Skiing time: 3–5 hours
High point: 2,200 feet

Total elevation gain: 1,200 feet
Best: November to April
USGS map: Seward D6

Chugach National Forest

For a delightful ski or snowshoe tour, try Turnagain Pass, which generally is buried in deep snow and is one of the few places with separate areas designated for skiers and snowmobilers. Winter was meant to be like this—snow crystals glinting in the sunlight or huge flakes falling softly among thick hemlock trees, towering snowy peaks, and, best of all, the rich silence of the mountains.

To reach the trailhead (elevation 1,000 feet), drive to mile 68 of the Seward Highway and the Turnagain Pass winter sports area, 59 miles south of Anchorage. The U.S. Forest Service has designated the west side of the highway for snowmobiles and the east side for nonmotorized winter sports. Access to the parking area for skiers and snowshoers, on the east side of the highway, is 0.2 mile south of the snowmobilers'

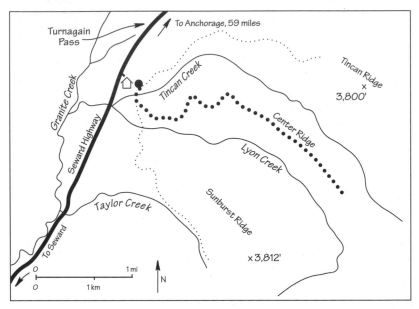

pullout (located west of the highway). Outhouses are provided at both parking areas.

On skis, there are several options. This book focuses on a tour up Center Ridge, the low hump that divides Tincan and Lyon creeks, but telemark skiers have made the higher mountains on either side of Center Ridge some of their favorite destinations.

Depending on previous ski traffic, the main trail may appear to head to the left, as you face away from the highway. This is the telemarkers' Tincan Ridge route. To access the easier Center Ridge route, head toward the gentle forested slope to the southeast—somewhat to the right—aiming for openings in the trees. Cross Tincan Creek en route, and look for markers on tree trunks indicating the trail. The route winds slowly uphill through conifer forest and natural meadows. Snow hangs heavily on the trees, creating myriad imaginary giants and monsters. After about a half mile, the route swings to the base of Center Ridge and climbs through a treeless area to the ridge crest. Trail markers end here. Do not continue along the base of the ridge below open snowy slopes; the slopes could avalanche from either side (see "Avalanches" in the Introduction).

Even a short trip winding through these snow-laden trees is an excursion into the best that Alaska's winters have to offer. Timberline, at about elevation 2,000 feet and 1½ miles from the parking area, makes a good destination for a short day. If time allows, continue on the crest of this rolling ridge, traversing along the north side of the higher knobs, until the route begins to climb toward a mountain peak. In midwinter the sun seldom reaches Center Ridge, so dress warmly. Fortunately, wind is unusual there. Jagged white mountain ridges rise all around, making this an unforgettable experience.

North of Center Ridge is the much higher Tincan Ridge. The Tincan Ridge trail is popular with telemark skiers. The route, which veers left shortly after leaving the parking area, often splits into several trails, but they converge to one before the route becomes truly steep.

On the opposite side of Center Ridge, to the right and beyond the point where the Center Ridge route enters the forest, is a less-used route into Taylor Creek or up what is known as Sunburst Ridge. If there is no previous track, pick your way from meadow to meadow up the hill and into this higher valley to the south.

Most skiers on both of these alternate routes use climbing skins on the bottoms of their skis for extra grip while ascending, and any existing tracks are likely to be too steep and frustrating for skiers without skins (this could be the case on Center Ridge, as well, so be prepared to break your own trail even if there is a good trail leaving the parking area). Above treeline, the alternate routes should be tackled only by experienced backcountry skiers trained in avalanche avoidance and rescue. Even some of them have been killed by avalanches on nearby mountain slopes. Before venturing out in the snowy Alaska mountains, take one of many interesting avalanche seminars offered to the public each winter (see "Avalanches" in the Introduction).

The east side of the Seward Highway from Bench Creek to Ingram Creek, including the Turnagain Pass area, is closed to motorized vehicles year-round.

Ski touring on Center Ridge, March

Portage to Potter

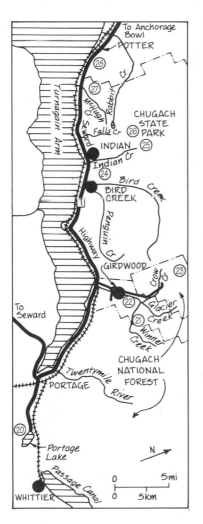

Red fox

BYRON GLACIER VIEW

Round trip: 1.6 miles
Hiking time: 1 hour
High point: 300 feet

Total elevation gain: 100 feet
Best: June to October
USGS map: Seward D5 SW

Chugach National Forest

This wide gravel trail is a delightful walk for families with small children, for Aunt Minnie, and for spry great-grandfather. An easy hike with no climbing, the trip is exciting for those who have never seen rugged mountain and glacier terrain up close. Bring a picnic lunch and relax in the heart of snow-and-ice country.

From Portage at mile 78.8 of the Seward Highway (48 miles south of Anchorage), drive a paved side road about 5½ miles east to Portage Lake. At the sign for the Begich Boggs Visitor Center take the right-hand fork 0.8 mile to the Byron Glacier trailhead parking area (elevation 200 feet). The continuing road leads another mile to the departure point for summer boat tours of Portage Lake.

On foot, follow the trail south to a fine view of Byron Glacier and snow-capped Byron Peak. The alders along the pathway make wonderful horses for young children to ride. Byron Creek, along the last half of the trail, is handy for throwing stones into; the vast quantities of stream-washed stones build into tottering towers and fortresses.

About a mile from the parking area, a large, permanent, inverted cone of snow is a remnant of avalanches that swept across the valley in previous winters; it is great for snow fights. Recently, this snow cone has opened sizeable crevasses and should be approached with caution. Unwary hikers could fall into the ice cave beneath the cone and into Byron Creek. The snow cone is beyond the end of the maintained trail; the route to reach it is rocky with several crossings of small streams.

Look on the snow cone for ice worms—black, less than an inch long, and slender as a thread. Yes, they really do exist! In the evening and

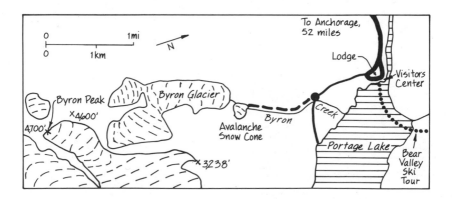

Byron Peak and Glacier, September (Photo: Helen Nienhueser)

on cool days, these tiny annelids, relatives of the earthworm, eat pollen and algae on the surface of the snow. Because they can live only near the freezing point of water, ice worms must escape from the heat of the sun or the subfreezing cold of winter. They do this by sliding into the snow or ice between crystal faces, an amazing little niche in the ecosystem.

Traveling onto the glacier itself is for experienced and properly equipped mountaineers only. Do not venture into ice caves or near towering ice faces, any of which can collapse.

Although summer temperatures are cooler than in Anchorage, the Byron valley is protected from the icy winds that blow across Portage Lake. Here the sun is warm. For camping, use one of the excellent Forest Service campgrounds along the entrance road. Considerable avalanche danger makes Byron valley unsafe during winter and spring (see "Avalanches" in the Introduction).

A good skiing or snowshoeing trip in the Portage Lake area is Bear Valley, which lies north of the lake. A road under construction in Bear Valley will alter access. If starting from the visitor center, head east across Portage Lake. Test to be sure the ice is thick enough; it should be at least 4 inches thick. Avoid potentially thin ice near the lake's outlet into Portage Creek and at the mouth of Placer Creek. Stay at least 100 feet from icebergs frozen into the lake. They often roll in the winter, breaking up the ice around them. If pressure ridges are present, watch for open water. Swing left into Bear Valley, and cross railroad tracks near the center of the valley. Stay away from the mountainsides to avoid avalanche danger. The width of the valley makes the center generally safe, but avoid it entirely during periods of extreme avalanche hazard. Do not travel near the ice cliffs of Portage Glacier; in winter the glacier calves from the bottom, sending waves that break up the lake near the glacier.

Byron valley, Portage Lake, and Bear Valley are closed to off-road vehicles year-round and to horses from April 1 through June 30.

21 WINNER CREEK GORGE

Round trip: 5.5 miles
Hiking time: 2–4 hours
High point: 600 feet
Best: Late May to October

Total elevation gain: 260 feet in,
200 feet out
USGS map: Seward D6 NW, NE

Chugach National Forest

A pleasant trail through tall spruce and hemlock trees at the base of Mount Alyeska leads to the plunging waters of Winner Creek gorge. Walk with history here on a portion of the old Iditarod Trail, which went from Seward over Crow Pass. Watch for moose and bears. The trail offers excellent ski touring.

At mile 90 of the Seward Highway (37 miles south of Anchorage), turn north onto Alyeska Highway and drive 3 miles to its end at a T intersection with Arlberg Avenue in the ski-resort town of Girdwood. Turn left, and follow Arlberg to its end at the posh Alyeska Prince Hotel. Park in the hotel lot (elevation 350 feet), and make your way on the hotel's trail network around either side of the hotel toward the mountain. To find the Winner Creek Trail, look for the tram cable exiting the hotel and disappearing up Mt. Alyeska. A Winner Creek Trail sign on the edge of the woods about 50 yards uphill from the tram terminal marks the route. At this point, cross under the cable and follow the trail into the forest.

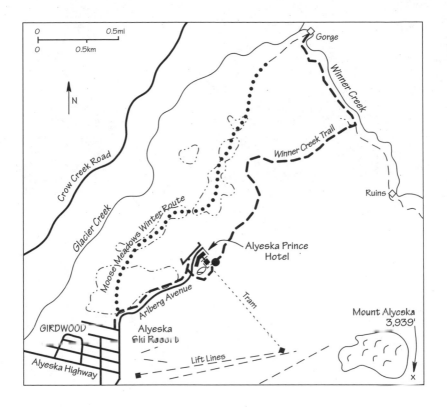

Under the trail's tall conifers, ferns, blueberry bushes, and moss carpet the forest floor. The trail crosses pleasant creeks and short sections of muskeg on bridges and boardwalks.

About 1¾ miles from the hotel, the hiking trail comes to a T-intersection above Winner Creek. Go left to Winner Creek gorge. The right branch goes toward the headwaters of Winner Creek, with bushwhacking access to Twentymile River and other intriguing areas.

The gorge (elevation 400 feet) is less than a mile away and is well worth the walk. A bridge over the gorge is a spray-in-your-face viewing platform over roiling water; the trail will eventually lead to Crow Creek Road. A side route cut through the trees (apparent as you approach the bridge) is a winter ski route but is too wet for summer walking.

The route to upper Winner Creek is narrow but reasonably good for more than a mile from the intersection. It passes a collapsed historic cabin. After the trail leaves the hemlock forest, the brush begins to close in. There is reasonable camping before the brush gets thick.

Winner Creek gorge, August

Bushwhacking is required beyond. Except for the upper reaches of Winner Creek, the trails are gentle with no severe ups or downs.

Winner Creek Trail makes good skiing, although it is not groomed. Check with the Ski Patrol about avalanche mitigation hazards. Upper Winner Creek is not recommended because of potential avalanches (see "Avalanches" in the Introduction). Most skiers, especially when snowfall is lean, prefer to ski the groomed Moose Meadows below the hiking trail, starting at the edge of Girdwood at the first curve in Arlberg Avenue. Park at Alyeska Resort, near the base of the chairlifts, or at the Alyeska Prince Hotel instead of along the street. These meadows connect with Winner Creek Trail to form a possible ski loop. As on any ski touring trail, be careful not to destroy the center ridge between the ski tracks, and please keep boots, snowshoes, and dogs off ski trails that others work hard to maintain.

Winner Creek Trail is closed to horses and off-road vehicles, including snowmobiles, year-round. The trail is managed by the U.S. Forest Service on an easement through state-owned land. Upper Winner Creek is in the National Forest.

22 GLACIER CREEK SKI TOUR

Round trip: up to 12 miles
Skiing time: 3–10 hours
High point: 800 feet
Best: December to February

Total elevation gain: 650 feet
USGS maps: Seward D6 NW, NE;
Anchorage A6

Municipality of Anchorage and Alaska Division of Land

To visit an intriguing canyon accessible only in winter, ski frozen Glacier Creek beneath towering snow-hung cliffs. Waterfalls, immobile cascades of ice, form trailside sculptures. Because the stream surface is smooth and climbs very gently, the trip is excellent for beginning skiers. Do not attempt the route on foot because of possible thin ice pockets.

At mile 90 of the Seward Highway (37 miles south of Anchorage), turn north onto Alyeska Highway and drive toward Girdwood 2.25 miles to Hightower Drive, which appears just before the bridge over Glacier Creek. Turn left, and continue north to the Girdwood school, leaving the car at the school parking area (elevation 150 feet).

On skis, head east toward the Mount Alyeska ski area, which is visible across the school yard. Pass through a gap in the trees at the far side of the playing field. Access to Glacier Creek is then to the right and down a small hill. Follow the creek upstream to the north. Certain portions of the creek near the school and the Alyeska Highway bridge seldom freeze over, while the canyon section of the creek will be solid, so give the route a try before deciding it is not possible. About 3 miles from the school, Winner Creek enters from the right in a frozen waterfall; shortly after, Crow Creek comes in from the left.

The skier has a river-level view of the canyon. Note the lovely hoarfrost crystals growing in ice caverns above open water. If time allows, continue up Glacier Creek beyond the entry of Crow Creek to The Narrows, the most scenic part of the canyon. Beyond The Narrows, the valley opens, with hanging glaciers and snowy peaks all around. These are the sources of Glacier Creek.

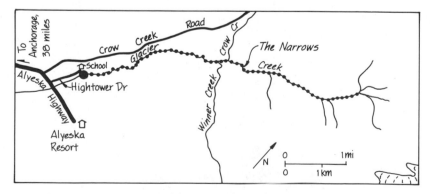

Dress warmly; the route is in the bottom of a canyon where sun seldom reaches in winter, and a cool breeze drains from the mountains almost anytime. A thermos of hot bouillon hits the spot at rest time on the trail.

This trip is suggested only for the coldest months when Glacier Creek is most likely to be well frozen; some years the weather is too warm for a good ice cover. On skis or snowshoes, weight is so well distributed that the danger of breaking through the ice is slight. Be cautious of thin ice, however, testing questionable spots first with a ski pole, then with a hard stamp of the ski. Generally the depth of the water beneath the ice is not great. If a ski trail is already established, snowshoers should make their own trails. Snowshoes break down the ridge between ski tracks, eliminating the advantage of a ski trail.

Ski touring on Glacier Creek, January

23 CROW PASS AND EAGLE RIVER TRAVERSE

Distance: to pass 8 miles round
trip; traverse 26 miles
Hiking time: round trip to Crow
Pass 4–6 hours, traverse 2–3 days
High point: 3,550 feet

Total elevation gain: 2,000 feet
northbound, 3,050 feet
southbound
Best: mid-June to September
USGS maps: Anchorage A6, A7

Chugach National Forest and Chugach State Park

The hike to Crow Pass offers a pleasant day trip into a beautiful mountain wilderness with gold mine relics, glaciers, alpine lakes, and wildflowers. Walk a dog sled route once traveled by mail carriers, explorers, and prospectors. Experienced hikers can take a 2- or 3-day point-to-point trip on the old Iditarod Trail through Chugach State Park to the Eagle River Nature Center.

In the early 1900s, the trail over Crow Pass was part of the Iditarod winter sled trail through the mountains between Turnagain Arm and Knik Arm, en route from Seward to Knik, thence to Interior goldfields. It was used alternately with Indian Pass Trail (trip 25), the preferred route. Steady use of both trails probably ended in the early 1920s when regular railroad service began between Seward and Fairbanks.

The old mail trail over Crow Pass continued down Raven Creek and out Eagle River. Today, this is a well-traveled hike popular on long weekends. It can be done faster; during the annual Crow Pass Crossing mountain run, top athletes manage the trail in 3–5 hours, despite its obstacles. Contact the Chugach State Park office for current trail information and to file a trip plan if desired (address in the Appendix).

To reach the Crow Pass trailhead, drive to mile 90 of the Seward Highway (37 miles south of Anchorage), and turn north onto Alyeska Highway. As the highway rounds a curve to the right at mile 2, turn left onto Crow Creek Road. Continue 5 miles to a bridge and, immediately

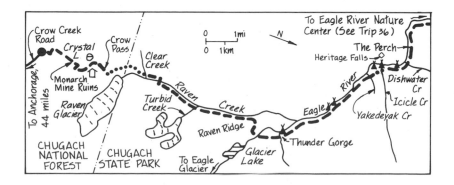

thereafter, a fork. Go right and uphill another mile to the road's end at the trailhead parking area (elevation 1,550 feet). The trail begins near the outhouse at the far end of the parking area. Reasonably priced van service for backpackers may be available in Anchorage and is especially helpful to those completing the traverse.

On foot, follow the old mining track as it climbs in switchbacks to brushline. At 2,500 feet elevation, 1.7 miles from the parking area, are the ruins of the Monarch Mine, a hardrock gold mine that operated from 1906 to 1948. The trail passes remains of what were once a mill and crew's quarters; above in the cliffs are mine adits. Maintaining elevation, walk along the hillside behind the mine ruins for a short side trip into the beautiful canyon through which Crow Creek cascades. Be sure to return to the trail switchbacks to continue upward; people have fallen trying to scramble off the path in this area, and using the trail will help prevent erosion.

To reach Crow Pass, follow the steep trail up the switchbacks above the mine ruins toward the pass. At mile 3 (3,500 feet elevation), a U.S. Forest Service A-frame cabin is available for public use. Make reservations through a Forest Service office (addresses in the Appendix). The cabin is not rented during winter and early spring because of avalanche hazard along the trail, and the cabin has no heating stove.

Nearby Crystal Lake nestles beneath a steep mountain wall and is rimmed by wildflowers in July and August. It is a splendid destination for many. West of the lake lies the tip of Crow Glacier. To see Raven Glacier, about a mile farther, hike north past the cabin, following rock cairns through the pass (elevation 3,600 feet). Look for Dall sheep and mountain goats.

Camping spots abound in both the mine and pass areas, although snow often persists well into June at the pass. Water is available. Campfires are not permitted. Snow showers and strong winds are possible any time, so take a parka, cap, and mittens. The trail is extremely hazardous in winter because of the avalanche danger (see "Avalanches" in the Introduction).

To complete the traverse to Eagle River, follow the trail and giant cairns from the Raven Glacier overlook down along the moraine bench on the southwestern side of the glacier. Cross Clear Creek (wading may be necessary at high water) at its junction with Raven Creek. In about ¾ mile, cross Raven Creek on a bridge over a gorge. Note the natural stone arch at the bottom of the waterfall in the gorge. From this point to the Eagle River Nature Center, hikers frequently sight black bears (see "Moose and Bears" in the Introduction).

The trail parallels the east side of Raven Creek for about 3 miles, staying on the hillside above the creek. Clear drinking water is not likely to be available in this stretch. Where the trail crosses Raven Ridge, there is a view of Eagle Glacier and, with binoculars, the area marked for fording Eagle River.

After the trail completes its steep descent to level ground at the base of Raven Ridge, it heads toward Eagle Glacier. A good river crossing area (elevation 850 feet) is well marked half a mile downstream from

Hikers, Raven Glacier near Crow Pass

Glacier Lake. Although instructions on how to ford are posted, practice crossing streams before taking on this swift glacial river (see "Stream Crossings" in the Introduction). Expect knee-deep water. Although of glacial origin, the river's water level does not rise greatly late in the day. Heavy rain, however, will cause the water level to rise rapidly; if the river is too high to cross safely, camp and wait.

From the ford, the trail generally parallels the river, passing Thunder Gorge in about 1½ miles. It is about 7 miles to Icicle Creek from the river crossing and about 13 miles to the Eagle River Nature Center and the trail's end (elevation 500 feet). The mountain walls make a fine backdrop along this stretch of trail. Near Dishwater Creek, the trail connects with trip 36, "The Perch." The path through the upper valley is narrow and has some tricky footing hidden by tall grass, but after descending from Crow Pass, the grades are mostly easy. The trail is subject to ongoing reconstruction to avoid areas where the river has undercut it. In one area, the route climbs a short ladder. Many good campsites appear along the way. Take a stove for cooking; campfires are permitted only in metal fire pits or on the gravel bars of upper Eagle River. Firearms may be carried for self-protection; target shooting is prohibited.

The entire trail is closed to off-road vehicles, including snowmobiles. The state park section of the trail is closed to horses and bicycles year-round. The portion in Chugach National Forest is closed to horses from April 1 through June 30 and is too steep for mountain bikes. The Eagle River Nature Center has a public pay phone and charges for parking.

2A BIRD RIDGE

Round trip: 2–12 miles
Hiking time: 1–8 hours
High point: 4,650 feet
Best: April to October

Total elevation gain: 4,600 feet
USGS maps: Seward D7 NW,
Anchorage A7

Chugach State Park

Take a picnic lunch in the spring, climb as high as you like, stretch out on the ground, and enjoy the warm sunshine and rich smell of earth—all while surrounding mountains remain cloaked in white. Because of its southern exposure, Bird Ridge sports the earliest spring flowers and is the standard spring conditioner for locals. The hike is steep but worth the effort because of its sweeping view of fjord-like Turnagain Arm.

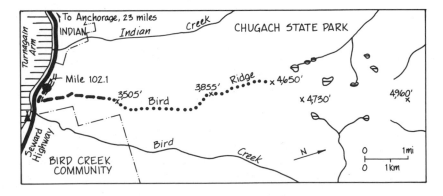

To reach the trailhead (elevation 50 feet), drive to mile 102.1 of the Seward Highway (25 miles south of Anchorage), and turn north into a large off-road parking area (marked).

The trail climbs through a pleasant birch forest to a boardwalk. Just beyond the boardwalk, turn left at the outhouses onto Bird Ridge Trail (marked). Follow the trail to the ridge crest and another trail sign. Ahead lie the valleys of Bird and Penguin creeks. The Bird Ridge foot trail continues left up the crest of the ridge.

You will soon leave brush behind. The first high point (elevation 3,505 feet) is about 2 miles from the trailhead, and is a good destination for a short trip. In early spring it may be necessary to skirt snow patches. The energetic can continue 4 miles farther to point 4650, overlooking the headwaters of Ship Creek. The ridge culminates at 4,960 feet. Several of the peaks beyond point 4650 are difficult and require mountaineering experience.

Whether you gain the high points or just stop at the powerline (400 feet), the views of the surrounding mountains and Turnagain Arm are magnificent. Turnagain Arm was named by Captain James Cook in 1778 when he explored these waters as part of his search for the Northwest Passage.

Bird Ridge, May (Photo: Ginny Hill Wood)

Turnagain Arm has one of the world's greatest tide differentials with a range of as much as 37 feet. Watch for tidal bores, the well-defined leading wave of an incoming tide. The Arm was scoured out by glaciers and has since been filled by silt carried by streams from the retreating rivers of ice. At low tide these mud flats are clearly visible. Because of the speed of the tide as it pours into and out of the narrow Arm and because of frequent high winds, the waters are dangerous for small boats.

Look for the season's first Jacob's ladders and anemones, followed by the flowering of the whole cycle of dry tundra plants. Ptarmigan and Dall sheep are frequent visitors to the ridge, and bald eagles ride the winds.

The footing is excellent, and though the hike is steep in spots, it is not unpleasantly so. No water is available along the trail. The best camping is at Bird Creek Campground; campfires are permitted only in the campground in metal campfire rings. Winter hiking on the ridge can be excellent, but stay on the ridge crest to avoid avalanches (see "Avalanches" in the Introduction) and avoid the overhangs of snow cornices on the leeward side of ridges. The trail is closed to off-road vehicles year-round.

25 INDIAN VALLEY

Round trip: 11 miles, traverse 21 miles
Hiking time: 5–7 hours, traverse 1–3 days
High point: 2,350 feet
Best: May to October, winter February to March

Total elevation gain: 2,100 feet to the pass, traverse 1,250 feet southbound
USGS maps: Seward D7 NW, Anchorage A7

Chugach State Park

Indian Valley offers a good family hike along Indian Creek through a delightful combination of forests and meadows to alpine tundra and tiny lakes high in the mountains. In the early 1900s, dog mushers drove their dog teams from Indian to Ship Creek. They crossed over Indian Creek Pass, a part of the Iditarod Trail system between Seward and Interior goldfields. The route over Indian Pass was used alternately with the route over Crow Pass (trip 23). The Indian Creek section of the trail has been cleared and is generally easy to find; the Ship Creek section is brushy, often boggy, and sometimes difficult to find. The traverse is most often done in winter by strong cross-country skiers.

To reach the trailhead, drive to the community of Indian, 25 miles south of Anchorage. At mile 103.1 of the Seward Highway, turn north onto a gravel road just west of a restaurant and Indian Creek. After 0.5 mile take the right fork and continue another 0.5 mile to the

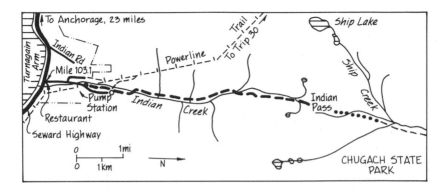

trailhead (elevation 250 feet), just before a powerline crosses the road. A pipeline carrying jet fuel from Whittier to Anchorage also crosses the road at this point. In 1993 a valve on the pipeline failed, and more than 35,000 gallons of fuel spilled, making it necessary to move the trailhead to this location. Spill cleanup activities are likely to last several years. The location of the trailhead could change after the cleanup project ends.

The trail begins on the left (west) side of the road and heads upstream along Indian Creek. After about a 5-minute walk, you will reach the old trailhead and a bridge. Do not cross the stream. The bridge leads to Powerline Trail (see trip 30). The trail to Indian Pass continues on the right-hand side of the stream. Follow this trail upstream through tall conifer trees and across delightful meadows created by winter avalanches. (Beware of these open places in winter and spring during periods of high avalanche danger. See "Avalanches" in the Introduction.) The trail can be wet and slippery; waterproof or well-greased boots with good traction are recommended. In late summer, the trail may be overgrown with tall grass in places. Ahead, high tundra beckons. The entire trail climbs gently with few steep ups or downs.

At the pass, knobs and dips formed by glacial action are today well vegetated by scrub hemlock and crowberries. Nearby ridges and side valleys with tiny alpine lakes invite exploration. Camping in the pass is lovely from mid-June through September, although there are few flat places. Water is available; campfires are not permitted, so bring a stove. For a longer trip, head for Ship Lake, about 3½ miles from Indian Pass. Walk over the pass and in about a mile bear left (southwest) up Ship Creek to the lake. This route connects with The Ramp (trip 30).

If you are planning to hike to the Ship Creek trailhead (15½ miles farther), check first with the Chugach State Park office for trail conditions and directions. Most of the trail is unmarked, and the lower end of the trail, going through bogs and vast areas of brush, is sometimes hard to find and requires bushwhacking in places. Traces of the old Iditarod Trail can still be found, however. Ruins of a roadhouse are on the west side of Ship Creek, about a mile above its confluence with the North Fork of Ship Creek. Watch for black bears in Ship Creek valley.

The usual place to ford Ship Creek is about half a mile downstream from the North Fork confluence. When the water level is high, this ford can be difficult for those with little experience in crossing rivers. Southbound hikers should find this site and take care to follow the center fork of Ship Creek to Indian Pass. A number of hikers and skiers have unwittingly followed the North Fork instead, a seriously wrong turn, and ended up in alder-choked Bird Creek canyon.

The Ship Creek trailhead (elevation 1,950 feet) is at mile 6.5 of Arctic Valley Road (see map of trip 34). Look for a bulletin board at the

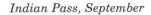

Indian Pass, September

parking area. A trail drops nearly to the level of the creek and then parallels the creek to Indian Pass. In winter, the 21-mile trip can take 3 days if extensive trail breaking is necessary, although if spring snow conditions are good, strong skiers can make the trip in 1 day (7–12 hours). For southbound skiers, the initial descent into Ship Creek Valley and the final descent into Indian Creek Valley may require short stretches of walking because of steep drops and moose holes. After mid-April, the segment that parallels Ship Creek may require frequent backtracking because of collapsed snow bridges across the creek. With a heavy pack, many skiers will have difficulty negotiating the tight turns descending through wooded Indian Valley. In the spring there will usually be a ski track set by someone familiar with the route (unless there is fresh snow).

Powerline Trail, described in trip 30, terminates in Indian Valley at the Indian Creek trailhead. It is open to mountain bikes. Do not attempt Powerline Trail in winter due to extreme avalanche hazard. Indian Creek Trail is closed to off-road vehicles, including bicycles, year-round.

26 FALLS CREEK

Round trip: 5.25 miles
Hiking time: 5–7 hours
High point: 3,000 feet

Total elevation gain: 2,900 feet
USGS maps: Anchorage A7,
Seward D7 NW

Chugach State Park

Climb a narrow, stream-cut valley, unusual for the Chugach Mountains, from the seaside to an alpine lakeshore. Less well known than other valleys near Anchorage, the Falls Creek valley leads quickly to alpine country, nicely framed views of Cook Inlet, and impressive rock outcrops and cliffs that rise above the lake.

To reach the trailhead, drive south on the Seward Highway to mile 105.6, 12.4 miles south of the Rabbit Creek Road interchange on the edge of Anchorage. A hiking sign alerts drivers that the trailhead is imminent. Find a small pullout next to Falls Creek, which tumbles out of the forest at the start of the trail.

Parts of the trail present some potential for confusion. The path starts to the right of the creek and stays to the right of it until near the end of the hike. Follow the main trail, roughly paralleling the creek, as it heads into the mountains. Don't cross the creek or parallel the highway.

Ten or 12 minutes after starting, the main route will leave the bluff just above Falls Creek and make a switchback to the right. Follow this, and continue steeply uphill through the forest, now away from the creek. The path pops out of the trees and levels briefly at a large rock. This is a natural spot to catch your breath and take in a bit of view.

Examine the trail carefully, as it forks here. Although the left fork descends slightly and seems narrower, it is the correct route. The right fork climbs directly and very steeply through alder to the rock face visible above and peters out.

The left fork is thankfully cut through thick brush as it works its way back to the creek. At occasional open spots, scan the cliffs above for sheep. The creek is a marvelous traveling companion, always there although it is going the other way. It jumps and tumbles its way downhill, one small waterfall after another. The trail soon leaves the alders in favor of grass and wildflowers, which in turn give way to tundra. The trail is less steep than it was near the beginning, and the valley is less V cut, showing instead a more typical U-shaped cross section that proves the glacial origin of the upper valley. This is a good lesson in geology, demonstrating the vast difference in how flowing water and ice carve away at the "solid" rock of mountains.

Ahead, the valley divides. The mountain tarn destination is in a higher valley to the left. The lower right-hand valley leads to the base

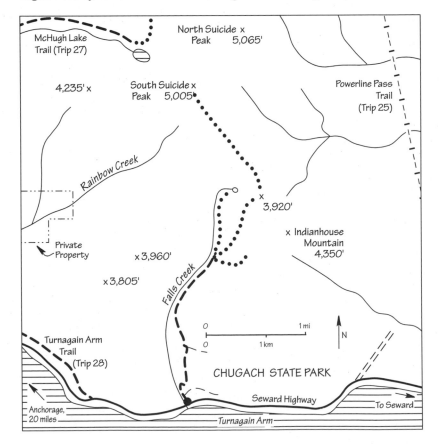

Headwaters of Falls Creek, October (Photo: Helen Nienhueser)

of Indianhouse Mountain (elevation 4,350 feet), the blocky cliffs of which are obvious as you walk up the valley. Between the forks, a ridge leads upward to far-reaching views from on high. This ridge also provides access, via the left-hand skyline, to the summit of South Suicide Peak (elevation 5,005 feet), a long ascent but one uncomplicated except for a steep stretch of talus slope.

To continue to the tarn, mount a short steep knob at the base of the dividing ridge. This knob, where the trail peters out, makes a nice destination in itself. To continue, hike left (north) over tundra into a small side valley and toward Suicide Peak. Flat areas in this side valley invite camping, although for most, this trip will be just a day hike. Follow this side valley about ⅔ mile until the valley dead-ends at a cirque and the lake. If you are alone and won't be bothering others, let go a yodel; the cliff faces all around will answer. Kick back in this south-facing reflector oven on fine days and enjoy the best of the Chugach Mountains.

27 McHUGH AND RABBIT LAKES

Round trip: 13 miles
Hiking time: 6–10 hours, or allow
  2 days
High point: 3,150 feet

Total elevation gain: 3,050 feet
Best: June to September
USGS maps: Anchorage A7, A8 SE

Chugach State Park

With its blue-black waters set below 2,000-foot walls of the Suicide
Peaks, Rabbit Lake is a scenic beauty. Smaller McHugh Lake is just
next door. The lakes make good destinations for an overnight or a long,
hard day hike. Camping is good, and there are several options for additional hikes and climbs from the lakes.

To reach the trailhead, drive to mile 111.9 of the Seward Highway,
6.4 miles south of the Rabbit Creek Road interchange on the southern
edge of Anchorage. Turn into McHugh Creek Picnic Area. Expect to
pay a fee for parking. Follow the McHugh entrance road uphill to the
back of the last and highest parking lot. The picnic area is closed with
a gate at 9 P.M.; alternate parking space is provided near the highway
for nighttime and early morning hikers.

The trail, marked "Turnagain Arm Trail" (trip 28), begins at the far
end of the parking area (elevation 100 feet). Follow the path about 150
yards to an intersection. Go left, following signs for "Potter" along
Turnagain Arm Trail. Within 10–15 minutes' walking time from the
parking lot, beyond two boardwalks and a mileage marker (mile 3 from

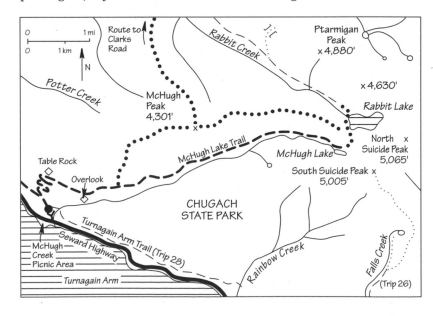

Potter), find McHugh Lake Trail (marked) heading to the right.

Follow this trail to the base of the hillside and up a long series of easy switchbacks to about 1,000 feet elevation. The rock outcrop above the trail is Table Rock, which affords grand views. (Pass below the rock outcrop cliffs and look for a steep side trail up to Table Rock. The silver waters of Turnagain Arm and Cook Inlet spread out to the horizon. An intermittent trail continuing uphill from Table Rock is a very steep route to the skyline ridge.)

The main McHugh Lake Trail passes Table Rock and enters the McHugh Creek valley, well above the creek itself. About an hour from the car, another small rocky outcrop appears on the right overlooking the creek, the Arm, the Kenai Mountains, and the parking lots far below. This is a good goal for those hikers with limited time or energy.

The main trail continues up the valley, traversing the hillside and gradually climbing. About 10 minutes from the overlook, a much steeper trail of loose gravel departs uphill to the left. This is a route to McHugh Peak. The main trail even-

Rabbit Lake, July (Photo: Pete Martin)

tually passes through the alder zone to a spectacular area of alpine tundra and tiny lakes surrounded by grand ridgelines and lofty summits. Snow remains at this elevation (near 3,000 feet) well into June. The first good camping is on a flat gravelly area to the right, below an obvious notch in the ridge across the valley. This is somewhat less than 2 miles from the lakes, where many more campsites are available.

McHugh Lake and the much larger Rabbit Lake lie at the bases of the Suicide Peaks (elevations 5,005 and 5,065 feet), which are separated by a high saddle called Windy Gap. On windless days, camping at lake level is delightful, and swimmers have been known to try the lakes. But Windy Gap is aptly named; winds can be fierce, so take warm clothes even in midsummer.

The Suicide Peaks have nontechnical routes, but neither is an easy ascent. Several other options for day hikes or alternate routes back to town will be more tempting for hikers. The most obvious is the low, easy ridge that separates the two lakes. Head westward up this ridge for better views or a trip to the summit of McHugh Peak (about 2¾ miles distant). Another 2–3 miles on, down the flanks of McHugh to the northwest, are possible exits on Clarks Road. There is no well-established trail. Scout a route to avoid clumps of alder. Clarks Road connects to upper Rabbit Creek Road.

Another hike is to walk about 1½ miles down Rabbit Creek valley from Rabbit Lake and then angle northward and uphill 700 vertical feet to Ptarmigan Pass (elevation 3,585 feet). The steep north side of this pass allows access to and from the South Fork of Campbell Creek, the Powerline Trail in that valley, and the Glen Alps entrance to Chugach State Park (see trip 30, "The Ramp"). Above this pass to the east is 4,900-foot Ptarmigan Peak. The Rabbit Creek side of the ridge from the pass to the peak is the easiest way up this steep mountain.

Although a trail continues down Rabbit Creek, a state court determined that it does not provide legal public access across private property. Chugach State Park, at this printing, had plans to bypass the property by constructing a new trail from Rabbit Lake along the southwest face of Flattop Mountain to the Glen Alps park entrance.

28 TURNAGAIN ARM TRAIL

One way: 9.4 miles
Hiking time: 5–8 hours
High point: 900 feet
Total elevation gain: 1,130 feet
   eastbound, 1,375 feet westbound

Best: April to November
USGS maps: Anchorage A8 SE;
   Seward D7 NW, D8

Chugach State Park

For an eagle's-eye view of Turnagain Arm, stroll Turnagain Arm Trail and find the first wild flowers of spring. Watch for white beluga whales and Dall sheep. The trail, originally developed in 1910 as a telegraph line, predates Anchorage and was used as an alternate mail trail from Seward to Knik when snow conditions necessitated. The main winter trails went over Crow Pass (trip 23) and Indian Pass (trip 25).

Turnagain Arm Trail offers opportunities for good family outings and can be hiked in short or long segments. South of McHugh Creek, during periods of new and full moons, watch for bore tides 45 minutes to an hour after the Anchorage low tide (check newspapers for tide times). Snow is seldom deep enough for skiing, so the trail often provides good winter hiking. Historically, the trail extended beyond Girdwood, but southeast of Windy Corner the trail is now obscured by natural land sloughing and highway construction. This description outlines a hike beginning at the north end of the trail. To start at other trail-

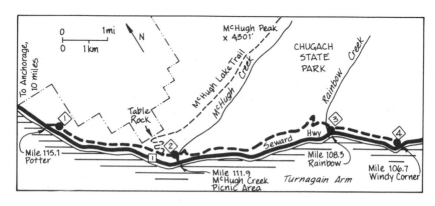

heads, see the westbound and shorter trip directions described later.

To reach the western trailhead near Potter Creek, drive to mile 115.1 of the Seward Highway, 2.7 miles south of the interchange at Rabbit Creek Road. Just south of Chugach State Park Headquarters (the historic Potter railroad section house), turn toward the mountains into the trailhead for Turnagain Arm Trail (marked) and park.

View from Turnagain Arm Trail (Photo: Pete Martin)

The Potter trailhead (1) (elevation 312 feet) is marked "Potter Creek." Portions of the trail are wet in spring. McHugh Creek Picnic Area (2) is 3.3 miles southeast (elevation gain 180 feet). About 10 minutes before McHugh, a trail branches off to the left. It leads to Table Rock and ultimately to McHugh and Rabbit lakes (trip 27).

At McHugh Creek Picnic Area (elevation 100 feet), follow the signs for Rainbow and the trail that bypasses the picnic area. To begin the hike at McHugh, drive to mile 111.9 of the Seward Highway. Follow the paved road to the lower parking lot, beside the creek. To walk to Rainbow, 4.2 miles away, follow the trail up the left side of the creek and cross a bridge. Just beyond the first switchback, a marked trail goes right to Rainbow (3) (elevation gain 800 feet). From McHugh Creek, the trail climbs high above Turnagain Arm, emerging from the cottonwood forest to a panoramic view. Here the trail passes under high, rocky, rotten cliffs. Be sure no one is on the cliffs above, watch for natural rockfalls, and take care not to dislodge rocks because people may be below. While the trail is safe enough, cliff scrambling here is dangerous; at least one person has been killed by losing his footing when scrambling up a slope of loose rock off the trail.

Beyond the cliffs the trail enters pleasant woods. There are side trails, but the main trail should be obvious. A little over 2 miles from McHugh, the trail again climbs, to about 900 feet and then descends in switchbacks, crossing the gravel Rainbow Valley road and continuing downhill along Rainbow Creek to the Rainbow trailhead at mile 108.3 of the Seward Highway.

From the Rainbow trailhead parking area, the trail climbs a gentle grade and continues 1.9 miles to Windy Corner (4) (elevation gain 200 feet). A short trail leads down to mile 106.7 of the Seward Highway.

Westbound Trips and Short Trips

McHugh Creek Picnic Area Access (2), mile 111.9 of the Seward Highway. To hike to the Potter Creek trailhead (3.3 miles, elevation gain 325 feet) take the left fork on the picnic area road to the upper parking area. The trail, which leaves from the upper end of the parking area, is marked.

Rainbow Valley Access (3), mile 108.3 of the Seward Highway. Park in the area provided north of the highway and east of Rainbow Creek. Walk west to the trailhead (marked) on the east bank of Rainbow Creek. McHugh Creek Picnic Area is 4.2 miles away (elevation gain 850 feet).

Windy Corner (4), mile 106.7 of the Seward Highway. Park at the pullout on the north side of the highway, and follow the trail up the boulder-covered slope to connect with the obvious old trail at the base of rock cliffs. Follow Turnagain Arm Trail west to Rainbow Valley (1.9 miles, elevation gain 200 feet).

The trail is closed to off-road vehicles year-round. Be alert for the occasional bear, especially during berry season, and especially between McHugh and Potter creeks.

ANCHORAGE BOWL

Dall sheep, Williwaw Lakes, trip 31 (Photo: Helen Nienhueser)

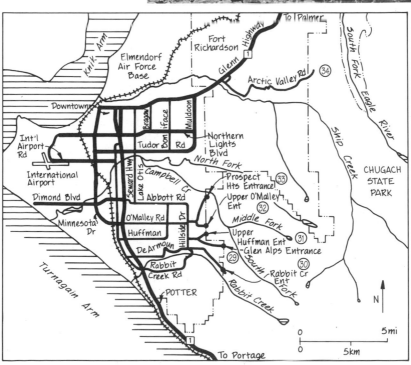

FLATTOP

Round trip: 3 miles
Hiking time: 2–5 hours
High point: 3,510 feet

Total elevation gain: 1,252 feet
Best: June to October
USGS map: Anchorage A8 SE

Chugach State Park and Anchorage Watershed

Thanks to easy access, Flattop is probably the most frequently climbed peak in Alaska, and the trip to the top has long been the classic afternoon hike near Anchorage. The view from the top extends from Denali (Mount McKinley) in the northwest to Mount Redoubt volcano in the southwest. Although parts of the climb are steep and over loose rock, most of the ascent is not difficult. Novices may have problems, however. Do not take small children unless they are cautious, experienced hikers. Boots with good traction and ankle support are needed for safety.

On the shortest and longest nights of the year, the Mountaineering Club of Alaska holds overnight outings on the summit despite the lack of water. Flattop is a good winter climb for those properly equipped, but avalanches have killed people here on the north and southwest slopes and even on the low hills leading up to Flattop. Do not slide down snow-filled gullies (see "Avalanches" in the Introduction, and check with the Chugach State Park office about current snow conditions before making a winter climb).

From the interchange of the Seward Highway and O'Malley Road in south Anchorage, turn uphill on O'Malley. Drive toward the mountains about 4 miles to the intersection with Hillside Drive. Turn right onto Hillside Drive, and continue 1 mile to Upper Huffman Road and a sign for Chugach State Park. Turn left, go 0.7 mile, and turn right onto Toilsome Hill Drive. (In winter, tire chains or four-wheel drive are recommended.) This road switchbacks steeply uphill for about 2 miles to the Glen Alps entrance to Chugach State Park. Park here (elevation 2,258 feet). Expect to pay a fee for parking.

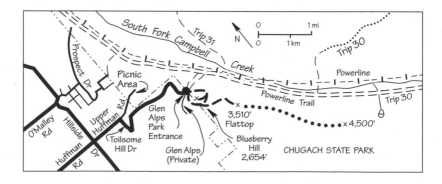

Turnagain Arm and Kenai Peninsula from Flattop, August (Photo: Helen Nienhueser)

The trail begins up an obvious stairway, winds through a grove of short mountain hemlock trees, and then emerges onto alpine tundra on the side of Blueberry Hill. Stay on the trail to protect the fragile vegetation. When the main trail forks, head right on the loop around Blueberry Hill, as directed by signs. This brings you to a saddle (elevation 2,500 feet) on the opposite side of Blueberry Hill. In winter, use caution, because the north-facing slope of this saddle becomes loaded with windblown snow, and hikers have triggered more than 80 avalanches here. At the saddle, the trail forks again. The left-hand fork continues around Blueberry Hill and rejoins the path you started on. The much steeper trail to Flattop is the right fork, which climbs to a second, higher saddle.

Parts of the next section of Flattop Trail are steep, exposed, and subject to falling rocks knocked loose by hikers or pets (do not take pets). In spring and early summer, parts of the route are covered by snow. When snowy, the last stretch to the top can be nearly vertical and should not be attempted without an ice ax. The top is, in fact, flat.

From Flattop (3,510 feet), the ridge can be followed 3 miles to its high point at 4,500 feet. The route is exposed in some places, but an experienced hiker will encounter no real difficulty.

Loose rock on the upper reaches of Flattop constitutes a serious potential hazard, and people have been injured here by falling rocks. Never roll rocks down the mountainside or allow children to do so. There may be people below, and even a small rock can become a lethal weapon. Avoid dislodging rocks, and if one accidentally falls, immediately yell "Rock!" at the top of your voice and continue yelling until the rock is at rest.

The trail is closed to motorized vehicles and bicycles year-round.

THE RAMP

Round trip: 12½ miles
Hiking time: 7–9 hours
High point: 5,240 feet

Total elevation gain: 3,000 feet
Best: June to September
USGS maps: Anchorage A7, A8 SE

Chugach State Park and Anchorage Watershed

On a sunny summer's day, take a delightful hike to "Ship Lake Pass," then climb a 5,240-foot peak. From the pass the mountainside does indeed resemble a ramp. The walk up is a moderately steep climb, gaining 1,200 feet elevation in about half a mile. From the top are fine views, especially of the Ship Creek headwaters. An easier summit is The Wedge (4,660 feet) southwest of the pass. The pass is a nice destination for a hike or a ski trip, and the trip to the pass makes a good hike for children.

From the interchange at the Seward Highway and O'Malley Road in south Anchorage, turn uphill on O'Malley Road. Drive O'Malley Road toward the mountains about 4 miles to its intersection with Hillside Drive. Turn right onto Hillside Drive, and continue 1 mile to Upper Huffman Road (there is a sign for Chugach State Park). Turn left, go 0.7 mile, and turn right onto Toilsome Hill Drive. (In winter tire chains or four-wheel drive are recommended.) This road switchbacks steeply uphill for about 2 miles to the Glen Alps entrance to Chugach State Park (elevation 2,258 feet). Park here; there is a parking fee.

On foot, follow the lower of two trails for half a mile to a powerline. (If biking, follow the right-hand or upper trail.) Turn right onto Powerline Trail and follow it about 2 miles, past 12 power poles, to a point where an obvious trail comes in from the left at a right angle. (The trip time can be shortened by riding a mountain bike to this point, but bicycles are not allowed off Powerline Trail.) Follow the trail downhill to the South Fork of Campbell Creek. Normally the stream can be crossed on rocks, but wading may be necessary at high water. The trail climbs the hill beyond the South Fork and continues through brush to cross

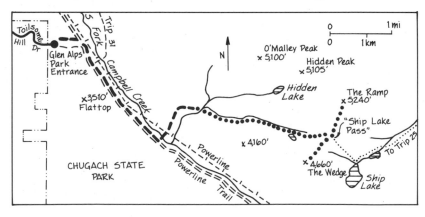

the stream draining the valley ahead. Wander up the valley on the south side of the main stream for easy, brush-free walking. The pass (elevation 4,050 feet, elevation gain 1,800 feet) is a fine destination, offering dramatic views of emerald-green Ship Lake and the mountains rising abruptly above it. From the pass it is a little over a half mile up the ridge to The Ramp to the north or The Wedge to the south.

Walking in this alpine valley is freedom itself. The brush has been left behind, and firm, dry tundra, laced with occasional springs, makes distances seem short. Look for wildflowers in season, ground squirrels, and Dall sheep. Enjoy the summer smell of heather on a warm sunny day. Visit Hidden Lake. Camping is inviting, but carry a cooking stove; campfires are prohibited in the park.

A 16-mile traverse from the Glen Alps trailhead to the community of Indian is possible via "Ship Lake Pass" (total elevation gain 1,900 feet). From the east side of the pass, descend steeply to Ship Lake (2,700 feet). Follow its outlet 1½ miles downstream, veer right around the toe of the ridge, and follow the center fork of Ship Creek upstream to Indian Creek Pass (elevation 2,350 feet). The trail from the pass to Indian is described in trip 25.

Another traverse to Indian Valley is 13 miles long over Powerline Pass (elevation 3,550 feet, elevation gain 1,300 feet), an easy walk or bike ride up Powerline Trail. From the pass, the trail switches back down the steep slope into Indian Valley. The trail ends at the trailhead for Indian Valley Trail (trip 25). The pass remains snowy into July, but when snow-free it offers good camping near the streams on its southeast side. The Campbell Creek drainage and the trail north of a metal gate, 2½ miles from Indian, are closed to motorized vehicles during snow-free months. Bicycles are allowed on the Powerline Trail. The descent to Indian is steep; therefore, some prefer to start at Indian and push bicycles uphill rather than ride down.

Ship Lake from The Ramp (Photo: Evan Steinhauser)

Skiing and snowshoeing in the Campbell Creek drainage are inviting, but the area is open to snowmobiles upstream of Middle Fork when snow cover is sufficient. Under the right conditions, any of the slopes could avalanche, and snow-filled gullies pose a serious hazard, even when surrounding slopes are bare (see "Avalanches" in the Introduction). The route over Powerline Pass should not be taken in winter due to extremely high avalanche hazard.

31 WILLIWAW LAKES

Round trip: 14 miles to first lake
Hiking time: 8–12 hours
High point: 2,600 feet
Total elevation gain: 1,585 feet
Best: June to early October
USGS maps: Anchorage A7;
   A8 NE, SE

Traverse: 18 miles
Hiking time: 2 days
High point: 3,700 feet
Total elevation gain: 3,550 feet
Best: June to early October
USGS maps: Anchorage A7;
   A8 NE, SE

Chugach State Park and Anchorage Watershed

Alpine gems all different in size, color, shape, and setting, the lakes at the base of Mount Williwaw (elevation 5,445 feet) lie in a mountain paradise. Walk amid a wide variety of alpine flowers on grassy meadows studded with scrub hemlock; pick blueberries, cranberries, and crowberries in season. Families with older children who are experienced hikers will enjoy this as an overnight trip. Or take the traverse past the Williwaw Lakes, over the pass, down the North Fork of Campbell Creek, then up the ridge over Near Point and back down the trail to the Prospect Heights entrance.

From the interchange at the Seward Highway and O'Malley Road in south Anchorage, turn uphill on O'Malley. Drive toward the mountains about 4 miles to Hillside Drive. Turn left, then immediately right onto

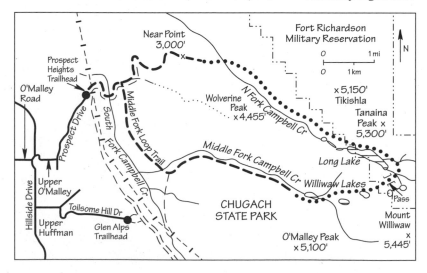

Long Lake, North Fork of Campbell Creek, August (Photo: H. Nienhueser)

Upper O'Malley Road. Follow it 0.5 mile to a T intersection. Turn left onto Prospect Drive (sometimes called Prospect Place), and continue 1 mile to a stop sign. Turn left, and drive 0.1 mile. Then turn right at the Prospect Heights entrance to Chugach State Park (elevation 1,115 feet). Expect to pay a fee for parking here.

On foot, follow the trail (an old homestead road) that heads east from the end of the parking area to a powerline. Turn left and continue on the main trail as it bends away from the powerline and descends to the South Fork of Campbell Creek. Cross a bridge, and continue around a sharp switchback and up a hill. At the top of the hill, take a sharp right-hand turn onto a side trail, Middle Fork Loop Trail. Follow this trail across the lower slopes of Wolverine a little less than 2 miles to a bridge across the Middle Fork of Campbell Creek. On the other side of the stream, the trail forks. Follow the left-hand fork (marked) about 3½ miles to the first lake. The right-hand fork goes to the Glen Alps entrance to Chugach State Park.

The first lake is a fine destination for a day trip or overnight and offers good camping nearby. If the weather is good, plan to linger here enjoying the magnificent scenery. For a slightly longer trip, continue upvalley about 1½ miles to the lake at 3,250 feet elevation, a beautiful lake in a cirque below Mount Williwaw. The pass to the North Fork of Campbell Creek is 500 feet higher and less than an hour away to the northeast.

A 2-day, 18-mile circular trip continues from the pass down to Long Lake and the valley of the North Fork of Campbell Creek. This valley can be followed around Long Lake (on either side of the lake) and past Tanaina, Tikishla, and Knoya peaks. Map-reading skills are essential to find the way out. This is a wonderful wilderness trip at Anchorage's back door. Because it is not easy to get to the North Fork valley, few people go there.

To complete the loop and return to the Prospect Heights entrance, follow the North Fork of Campbell Creek downstream about 2½ miles beyond the last lake. Begin climbing up the northwest ridge of Wolverine Peak on your left before there is much brush. Aim for a notch in the ridge southeast of a bump called Near Point. It is a steep climb with about 800 feet of elevation gain. Once on top, follow the ridge over Near Point and pick up a narrow trail that descends from Near Point to the end of the old homestead road. Follow it back to the Prospect Heights entrance to the park.

It is possible to make the trip to Williwaw Lakes from the Glen Alps entrance to Chugach State Park. That route is about 1½ miles shorter, one way, but is quite wet in spots. The walking from the Prospect Heights entrance is much better. For directions to the Glen Alps entrance, see the description for The Ramp (trip 30). From the Glen Alps parking lot, walk to Powerline Trail, turn right, and continue for about 300 yards. Take a trail to the left (marked with a sign for Middle Fork Loop Trail) that leads downhill to the South Fork of Campbell Creek. Cross the stream on a bridge and follow a trail north (left), more or less paralleling the stream. In about 1½ miles is the fork in the trail above the Middle Fork of Campbell Creek. Follow the right-hand trail to Williwaw Lakes.

Campfires are prohibited in the park, so bring a stove. The trip to Williwaw Lakes also makes a good ski trip with access via Middle Fork Loop Ski Trail from either the Glen Alps or the Prospect Heights entrance. Be aware of avalanche danger (see "Avalanches" in the Introduction). The Glen Alps route is closed to bicycles. The trail from Prospect Heights is open to bicycles on the old homestead road to its end at the base of Near Point (2.4 miles). The entire area north of the Middle Fork is closed to motorized vehicles year-round. The Campbell Creek drainage upstream (south) of Middle Fork is open to snowmobiles when snow cover is sufficient.

32 WOLVERINE PEAK

Round trip: 11 miles
Hiking time: 6–9 hours
High point: 4,455 feet
Total elevation gain: 3,340 feet

Best: June to September; winter,
November to April
USGS maps: Anchorage A7, A8 NE

Chugach State Park and Anchorage Watershed

Wolverine, the broad triangular mountain on the skyline east of Anchorage, makes an excellent 1-day trip, offering views of Anchorage, Cook Inlet, and the Alaska Range and glimpses of the lake-dotted wild country behind the peak. An old homesteader's road, now part of the Chugach State Park trail system, makes a fine access to timberline for hiking and ski touring. Watch for ground squirrels, spruce grouse, moose, and, on rare occasions, a wolverine. Pick blueberries and cranberries in season.

From the interchange at the Seward Highway and O'Malley Road in south Anchorage, turn uphill on O'Malley. Drive toward the mountains about 4 miles to Hillside Drive. Turn left, then immediately right onto Upper O'Malley Road. Follow it 0.5 mile to a T intersection. Turn left onto Prospect Drive and continue 1 mile to a stop sign. Turn left, and drive 0.1 mile to the Prospect Heights entrance to Chugach State Park (elevation 1,115 feet). Expect to pay a fee for parking here.

Wolverine Peak from Anchorage, October

On foot, follow the trail (an old road) that heads east from the parking area to a powerline. Turn left, and continue on the main trail as it bends away from the powerline and descends to the South Fork of Campbell Creek. Cross a bridge and continue around a sharp switchback and up a hill. A side trail (an old road) that turns sharply right is Middle Fork Loop Trail. Continue past this trail to the next trail (again an old road) entering from the right, a

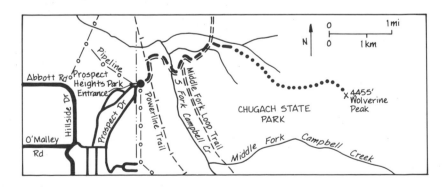

little over a mile beyond the creek and 2⅓ miles from the parking area.

Follow this trail as it angles off uphill, starting at an elevation of 1,330 feet. The distance from here to the peak is about 3 miles. The trail narrows to a footpath through blueberry bushes, then emerges above brushline, paralleling the north side of the ridge crest. Climb to the crest and continue to the peak. The summit (elevation 4,455 feet) is not obvious much of the way. The hike to brushline is a pleasant evening outing with a fine view of Denali (Mount McKinley).

Climbers may want to tackle the peak in winter, although some avalanche hazard may exist (see "Avalanches" in the Introduction). The upper slopes are likely to be windpacked or windswept, and crampons may be necessary. The last part of the climb generally does not have enough snow for skiing.

A network of about 20 miles of ski trails is accessible from Prospect Heights and three other entrances to Chugach State Park. Ski the old road to its end beyond the Wolverine turnoff or take Middle Fork Loop Trail. The Loop Trail connects this entrance with Upper O'Malley, Upper Huffman, and Glen Alps park entrances and can be skied as a circular trip using the Powerline Trail. Maps of the trail system are available from the park office (address in the Appendix) and are posted at trailheads.

The area is closed to motorized vehicles year-round. Bicycles are allowed on the main trail, from Prospect Heights to the turnoff to Wolverine and beyond to the overlook at the north end of the homestead road (2.4 miles), the base of Near Point (see trip 33).

33 NEAR POINT AND TIKISHLA PEAK

NEAR POINT
Round trip: 8.5 miles
Hiking time: 4–5 hours
High point: 3,000 feet
Total elevation gain: 2,000 feet
Best: late June to September
USGS maps: Anchorage A7, A8 NE

TIKISHLA PEAK
Round trip: 18 miles
Allow 2 days
High point: 5,150 feet
Total elevation gain: 5,000 feet
Best: late June to September
USGS maps: Anchorage A7, A8 NE

Chugach State Park, Anchorage Watershed, and Fort Richardson Military Reservation

Two climbs—one easy, one long and hard—begin with the same access. Lower, closer, and easier, Near Point is a knob overlooking east Anchorage. It is a classic hike, suitable for summer evenings. Tikishla Peak is across the North Fork of Campbell Creek from Near Point. Because the North Fork valley has difficult access, Tikishla sees very little traffic. Hikers may wish to forego the climb of Tikishla and explore the valley, perhaps connecting with trip 31, "Williwaw Lakes," to make a loop back to their starting point via the Middle Fork of Campbell Creek.

The primary access to these destinations is via O'Malley Road in south Anchorage. For access that is convenient to east Anchorage but is more complex and harder to find, see the end of this description. For the main access, find the interchange at O'Malley Road and the Seward Highway, and turn east. Drive about 4 miles up O'Malley Road to its intersection with Hillside Drive. Turn left then immediately right onto Upper O'Malley Road. Follow it 0.5 mile to a T intersection. Turn left onto Prospect Drive, and continue 1 mile to a stop sign. Bear left, and go 0.1 mile to the Prospect Heights entrance to Chugach State Park (elevation 1,115 feet). Expect to pay a fee for parking here.

Tikishla and North Fork Campbell Creek, September (Photo: Helen Nienhueser)

Near Point

On foot, follow Near Point Trail (an old homesteader's road) that heads east from the parking area to a powerline; turn left and continue on the main trail as it curves away from the powerline and descends to the South Fork of Campbell Creek. Cross a bridge, and continue on the old road (now a wide path) to its end at the base of Near Point, 2.4 miles from the parking area. Ignore trails branching to the right.

Near Point (elevation 3,000 feet) is an intermediate high point on a low ridge. A narrow footpath (marked) winds up its west side. This path is wet in a few spots and can be slippery. Avoid making ever-wider trails around muck holes, and resign yourself to dirty shoes in the interest of reducing the rate of erosion. Once past the brush, the trail is dry and pleasant, if steep, to the top. This climb could be a good first summit for a youngster, especially one who would enjoy the bicycle ride along the initial 2.4 miles before the climb. Only this initial, relatively wide and flat part of the trail is open to mountain bikes.

Tikishla Peak

To reach Tikishla, climb to the top of Near Point and continue along its ridge. The trail peters out, but follow the ridge down to a low point and then drop off the ridge into the valley of the North Fork of Campbell Creek. Tikishla Peak is the mountain across the valley and a little upstream. Angle upvalley as you descend to avoid mountain hemlock and brush directly below. Aim more or less for the base of an inviting ridge that rises from the creek to the summit of Tikishla. Once at the creek, it is about 3,000 feet of climbing up the ridge to the summit of Tikishla (elevation 5,150 feet). For most, this trip is probably best as an overnight, with camping near the base of Tikishla Peak. Carry a stove, because campfires are not permitted.

From the top of Tikishla, it is possible to walk the main ridge northwest to Knoya Peak (elevation 4,600 feet) before dropping back into the valley. There are several other variations on this trip, as described in the following.

East Anchorage Access to Near Point

From Tudor Road in east Anchorage, turn south on Campbell Airstrip Road and proceed until you pass under a powerline. Park, and walk away from the city on the hilly powerline trail to Campbell Creek Canyon. Turn left, and follow a footpath along the edge of the canyon and gradually uphill to Near Point Trail. At minor intersections, go uphill. At the one major intersection, go right. These trails are unmaintained and unmarked; it is possible to become lost.

East Anchorage Access to Tikishla Peak

Another route to Tikishla is via a bump sometimes called "Baldy." It is more hill than mountain but rises above treeline and has a fine view. The trail to Baldy is on Fort Richardson military reservation land, and the Army requires that hikers call the military police (phone number in the Appendix) to get permission and be sure there will be no military maneuvers in the area.

To find the trail to Baldy, start from mile 2.4 of Campbell Airstrip Road in Far North Bicentennial Park. Park on the left (north) side of the road, and hike or bike from a red gate across the base of the mountains on a wide old army tank road. En route, you will cross a major powerline, enter military land, and step gingerly on a rotting bridge over the North Fork of Campbell Creek.

Take a right fork beyond the creek. Ignore smaller trails joining or diverging until you have gone nearly 2 miles from Campbell Airstrip Road. There, at the first right beyond the bridge (a 7–10-minute walk past the bridge), find a narrower, unmarked 4-mile trail that twists and winds uphill through wonderful forest to Baldy. This trail roughly parallels the North Fork of Campbell Creek (often at some distance) and then enters steep switchbacks. To continue 3 more miles beyond Baldy to Tikishla, hike up the ridge over Knoya Peak, and climb on to Tikishla. This is about 18 miles round trip.

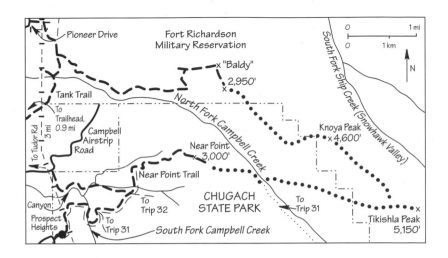

The trail to Baldy is also accessible from the Chugach Foothills subdivision. Take East 36th Avenue east from Muldoon Road, turn right on Pioneer Drive, and follow it 0.5 mile to a drainage culvert near 8450 Pioneer. There, a trail follows the drainage ditch upstream between houses to U.S. Army Reservation land. Go right, and follow a powerline to a major four-way intersection of powerlines. At this intersection, go left toward the mountains along a powerline, and pick up a distinct path through the woods. It lets hikers out on the tank trail. Go right, and follow the tank trail about 5 minutes. Then go left on the trail to Baldy.

The tank trails are perfect for mountain bikes, but on the Baldy trail all wheeled vehicles are forbidden. Parking is limited and awkward in the residential neighborhood. Park a couple of blocks away if necessary to avoid crowding residents.

34 RENDEZVOUS PEAK

Round trip: 3.5 miles **Total elevation gain: 1,500 feet**
Hiking time: 2–5 hours **Best: anytime**
High point: 4,050 feet **USGS maps: Anchorage A7, B7 SW**

Chugach State Park, Anchorage Watershed, and Fort Richardson
Military Reservation

To introduce children to mountains, Rendezvous Peak is a perfect first summit. Adults will enjoy the pleasant, easy climb, and there are spectacular views of Denali (Mount McKinley), Mount Foraker, Mount Susitna, Cook Inlet, Turnagain and Knik arms, Anchorage, and the

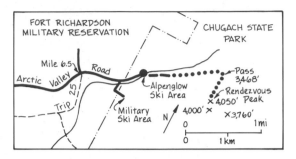

valleys of Ship Creek and Eagle River. In winter, when snow conditions are good, the trip to the pass is fun on cross-country skis.

From Sixth Avenue and Gambell Street in Anchorage, drive northeast on the Glenn Highway 6.3 miles and take the exit for Arctic Valley Road. Southbound traffic should take the exit for Fort Richardson at mile 8.1 of the Glenn Highway, and follow signs to Arctic Valley. Drive 7 miles to the end of the gravel road at Alpenglow Ski Area. Stay on the main road; do not take a right-hand fork near the ski area. In winter studded tires, four-wheel drive, or chains may be required for the steep ascent to Arctic Valley. From the parking lot (elevation 2,550 feet), walk on the right-hand side of the stream up the valley to the northeast. A footpath leads to the pass.

The pass (elevation 3,468 feet) has fine views, but those from the top of Rendezvous Peak (elevation 4,050 feet) are even better. A steep but

South Fork of Eagle River from Rendezvous Peak (Photo: Gayle Nienhueser)

short ascent up the ridge to the right (south) of the pass leads to the craggy summit. Sit for a while to enjoy the view. From the top, the ridge extending southeast beckons, promising a walk in the clouds high above the valleys of Ship Creek and the South Fork of Eagle River. Be sure to carry water if you go very far.

From Rendezvous Peak choose your own descent route. In winter stay on windblown ridges to minimize avalanche hazard (see "Avalanches" in the Introduction).

A one-way trip is possible from Arctic Valley to the South Fork of Eagle River. From the summit of Rendezvous, follow the ridge southeast about 2 miles toward the head of the South Fork valley, climbing over or around three more "summits": 4,000,

Sliding down the heather on Rendezvous peak, circa 1970. (This was in the days before sliding on heather was seen as damaging to the environment.)

3,760, and 3,855 feet. From the last peak, descend to the low, 2,900-foot pass between the Ship Creek and Eagle River drainages. From the pass, descend the steep hillside about half a mile to the South Fork trail, an elevation loss of about 800 feet. As you descend, head for the place where a gravel road crosses the creek. When you intersect the trail, turn left to reach the trailhead, less than a half mile away. See trip 35, "Eagle Lake," for driving directions to the trailhead.

Because the access to Rendezvous Peak is on military land and subject to military control, civilian travel occasionally may be restricted due to weather or military training. Generally, no problems are encountered. Alpenglow Ski Area buildings and equipment are private property. Please respect them, and report any vandalism. The area is closed to off-road vehicles year-round.

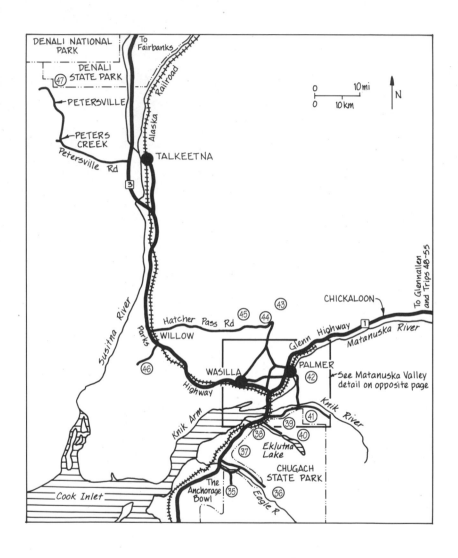

DENALI NATIONAL PARK

DENALI STATE PARK

47

PETERSVILLE

PETERS CREEK

Petersville Rd

To Fairbanks

Alaska Railroad

TALKEETNA

3

Susitna River

Hatcher Pass Rd

45

44

43

Parks

WILLOW

46

Highway

WASILLA

Knik Arm

CHICKALOON

Glenn Highway

1

Matanuska River

To Glennallen and Trips 48-55

PALMER

42

See Matanuska Valley detail on opposite page

Knik River

41

39

40

38

Eklutna Lake

37

CHUGACH STATE PARK

The Anchorage Bowl

35

Eagle R

36

Cook Inlet

0   10 mi
0   10 km

N

Opposite: *Bull moose*

NORTH OF ANCHORAGE

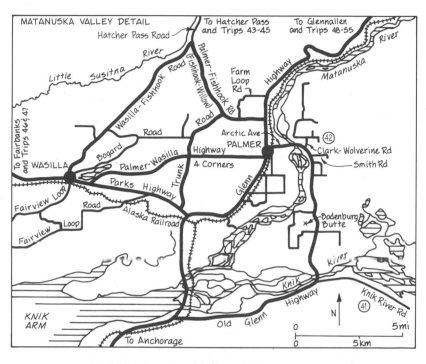

MATANUSKA VALLEY DETAIL

To Hatcher Pass and Trips 43-45
To Glennallen and Trips 48-55
Hatcher Pass Road
Little Susitna River
Wasilla-Fishhook Road
Palmer-Fishhook Road (Fishhook-Willow)
Farm Loop Rd
Matanuska River
To Fairbanks and Trips 46 & 47
Bogard Road
Arctic Ave
PALMER
Highway
42
Clark-Wolverine Rd
Smith Rd
WASILLA
Palmer-Wasilla
Highway
4 Corners
Parks Highway
Trunk
Glenn
Fairview Loop
Road
Alaska Railroad
Bodenburg Butte
Fairview Loop
River
KNIK ARM
Knik
Old Glenn
Highway
Knik River Rd
41
To Anchorage
N
0   5mi
0   5km

35 EAGLE LAKE

Round trip: 9–11 miles **Total elevation gain: 750 feet**
Hiking time: 4–8 hours **Best: June to early October**
High point: 2,650 feet **USGS map: Anchorage A7**

Chugach State Park

For a backcountry treat, visit the valley of the South Fork of Eagle River. Head for shimmering, glacier-fed Eagle Lake, then wander through meadows of alpine flowers to nearby clear-water companions. Beyond lies a wilderness of rugged mountain peaks. Eagle Lake is an easy day trip, but more than a day is needed to explore this lovely valley.

From the Muldoon Road interchange on the Glenn Highway on the northeast edge of Anchorage, drive 7 miles out of town on the Glenn Highway to the Eagle River Loop Road/Hiland Road exit. Turn right onto the road coming across the overpass (South Eagle River Loop Road), and in 0.1 mile turn right on Hiland Road (also known as Hiland Drive). Southbound traffic should cross the freeway overpass on South Eagle River Loop Road to the east side. Drive 3.5 miles on Hiland Road to the end of state maintenance, take the right-hand fork, and after another 1.5 miles take another right fork, staying on Hiland Road. After 0.4 mile, go left, following Hiland Road downhill and across the South Fork of Eagle River. Continue another 1.5 miles past the creek, turn right onto South Creek Road (marked). Follow it across the river, and turn right onto West River Drive. The park entrance is on the left (elevation 1,900 feet).

Past access problems in this valley have caused conflicts between landowners and hikers or skiers. Respect private property and use the Chugach State Park access only. Park at the edge of the road. There is very limited parking available. In winter, Hiland Road becomes icy and a four-wheel-drive vehicle may be needed.

The trail begins as a boardwalk and then climbs to and follows a bench for about a mile. The trail then descends to a bridge across

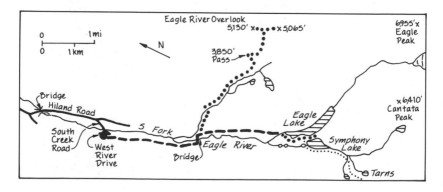

Eagle Lake and Eagle Peak, July (Photo: Helen Nienhueser)

South Fork (about 2 miles from the trailhead). Once across the creek, follow the trail across the valley, then up the east side of the valley to Eagle Lake, about 9 miles round trip from the trailhead. Some spots in the trail are wet.

From Eagle Lake (elevation 2,600 feet), hikes and climbs abound. Some boulder-hopping is necessary to reach Symphony Lake (elevation 2,648 feet), 11 miles round trip from the trailhead. Symphony Lake and the tarns above it are fine destinations. Extend this trip, if you like, into the valley behind Symphony Lake or around the south side of Eagle Lake. These valleys have no trails, and some bushwhacking is necessary. The two tarns high above and behind Symphony Lake are pretty, and the ridge between the tarns leads to a high plateau (elevation 4,500 feet) overlooking the North Fork of Ship Creek. Challenging peaks in the area, for experienced mountaineers only, include Cantata (6,410 feet), Calliope (6,810 feet), and Eagle Peak (6,955 feet).

A side trip for another day is Eagle River Overlook. From the park entrance, follow the trail across the bridge and across the valley. When the trail turns south toward Eagle Lake, continue straight up the slope to a hanging valley above. Follow game trails through brush, and cross the creek when you can.

About 2½ miles from the South Fork, climb the steep, grassy slope on the left to a pass at 3,850 feet. From here, stroll to points 5065 and 5130 ("Overlook"), both of which provide spectacular views of Eagle River valley and the mountain wilderness beyond. From the park entrance to the overlook is about 12 miles round trip.

Camping is unrestricted on park lands, but campfires are not permitted; take a stove. Watch for moose, black and grizzly bears, Dall sheep, and raptors, including merlins. Chugach State Park lands in the South Fork drainage are closed to off-road vehicles year-round.

36 THE PERCH

Round trip: 8 miles
Hiking time: 4–6 hours
High point: 800 feet

Total elevation gain: 300 feet
Best: May to October
USGS maps: Anchorage A6, A7

Chugach State Park

Put a picnic in the knapsack, and stroll to The Perch through a wooded canyon with 6,500-foot mountain walls shooting skyward all around. This well-maintained trail is a good family hike anytime but is especially welcome in early spring or late fall when other hikes are closed by snow. The route lies along the historic Iditarod Trail, which runs between Seward and the Interior goldfields. Ambitious backpackers can follow it well beyond The Perch to Crow Pass, 26 miles distant (see trip 23).

From the Muldoon Road overpass on the Glenn Highway at the northeast edge of Anchorage, drive east 7 miles on the Glenn Highway, and take the Eagle River Loop/Hiland Road exit. At the first light, bypass Hiland Road and continue on Eagle River Loop Road 2.6 miles until the highway crosses Eagle River and comes to a major intersection at Eagle River Road. Turn right, and proceed 10.8 miles to the road's end at the Eagle River Nature Center. Expect to pay a fee for parking; this is not included in State Parks' seasonal pass.

The trail starts at the back side of the Nature Center (elevation 500 feet) and is marked Iditarod Trail. Check the public information bulletin board before starting on the trail—when bears fish for salmon in

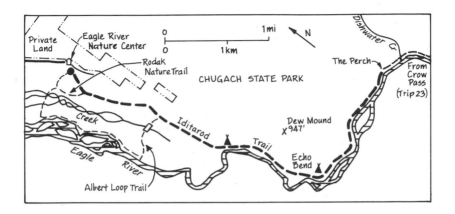

streams near the trail, a cautionary notice is posted. Two forks to the right are the two ends of the Rodak Nature Trail, a ⅔-mile loop. The first fork also accesses the 3-mile Albert Loop Trail. These forks are well marked, and the main route is obvious. At mile 1, there is another crossroads, where the Albert Loop Trail rejoins the main route. For The Perch, continue straight through this intersection.

The main trail wanders through birch and spruce; lichens and mosses cover the rocky ground. The cliffs of Dew Mound are visible to the left. About 2 miles from the visitors center, the trail begins to follow the river closely and, about 3 miles out, reaches a pleasant viewpoint and campsite beside the river at Echo Bend. Continue another mile to The Perch (marked), a massive, smooth rock outcropping. With a fine view up the Eagle River canyon to the snowy glaciated peaks beyond, this is the perfect spot for a photo and a sandwich. Eagle, Polar Bear, and Yukla peaks rise overhead to 7,500 feet and are among the most impressive peaks to be found along a trail in southcentral Alaska.

The energetic may want to extend their walk another 1½ miles to a view of lovely Heritage Falls on the south side of Eagle River. The less energetic may wish to stick near the Nature Center. The Rodak Nature Trail includes a salmon-viewing platform that doubles as a mountain-viewing and sunning deck. The Albert Loop Trail leads to the gravelly banks of Eagle River in about 45 minutes and comes back by a different route.

Reach the Albert Loop Trail by taking the first right-hand fork for the nature trail. The wide path leads downhill. When it bends left and begins to level off, continue straight ahead on a much narrower footpath—the Albert Loop route (note that some park maps still show an old variation of this access). If water is high in the river, you may have to cross small overflow channels on logs or get your feet wet. A self-guided geology tour is available by asking for a pamphlet in the Nature Center.

Along any of these popular trails, open fires are generally not allowed. Along the Iditarod Trail, fires are permitted only in metal fire

Eagle River near The Perch, November

pits at Rapids Camp (mile 1.7) and Echo Bend (mile 3.0). The park encourages campers to sleep away from these fire pits, because the food odors around the pits attract black bears. Camp stoves are generally better for cooking.

These trails can be skied in winter when there is enough snow to cover the rocks. After the river freezes, it makes a grand ski highway. Check with park rangers for ice conditions, then follow either end of the Albert Loop Trail to the river. All trails mentioned here are closed year-round to horses, other pack animals, mountain bikes, snowmobiles, and other vehicles.

37 ROUND TOP AND BLACK TAIL ROCKS

MEADOW CREEK ACCESS
Round trip: 8 miles to Black Tail Rocks, 10 miles to Round Top
Hiking time: 6–8 hours
High point: Round Top 4,755 feet
Best: June to September
Total elevation gain: 2,750 feet to Black Tail Rocks, 3,470 feet to Round Top
USGS maps: Anchorage B7 SW, SE

LITTLE PETERS CREEK ACCESS
Round trip: 11 miles to Round Top, 13 miles to Black Tail Rocks
Hiking time: 7–10 hours
High point: Round Top 4,755 feet
Best: June to September
Total elevation gain: 4,500 feet to Round Top, 5,000 feet to Black Tail Rocks
USGS maps: Anchorage B7 NW, SW, SE

Chugach State Park

A panoramic view from Mount Redoubt volcano to Denali (Mount McKinley) rewards the hiker who makes the steep climb to Round Top's summit. All around are the Chugach Mountains, including Bold Peak in the Eklutna area, the high Chugach behind it, and Eagle and Polar Bear peaks in the Eagle River area. This easy day outing takes the urban dweller into an alpine wonderland.

Two approaches are possible: via Meadow Creek and via Little Peters Creek (also called Ptarmigan Valley). Meadow Creek offers the most elevation gain by car but crosses private land; call Chugach State Park for current access information (phone number in Appendix). The

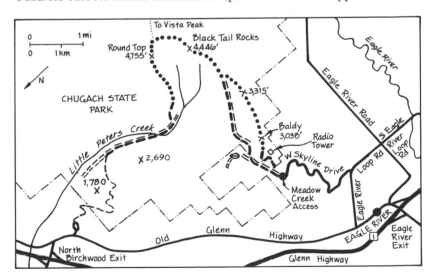

Ptarmigan Valley Trail is longer and gains more elevation on foot and offers pleasant forest at its lower end.

Meadow Creek Access

From the Muldoon Road overpass on the Glenn Highway at the northeast edge of Anchorage, drive 7 miles on the Glenn Highway to the Eagle River Loop/Hiland Road exit. Turn right onto the road (South Eagle River Loop Road) coming across the overpass. Follow Loop Road for 3.4 miles to West Skyline Drive on the right (just before Loop Road turns left).

Southbound traffic should take the second exit for Eagle River and cross to the east side of the freeway. From the first stoplight, drive 0.7 mile on the Old Glenn Highway to Eagle River Loop Road; turn right. In 1.1 miles, where Loop Road bears right, turn left onto West Skyline Drive.

Follow West Skyline Drive (also known as Skyline Drive) 2.4 miles to a gate and park (elevation 1,700 feet). The name of the road changes several times. Stay on the paved road until its end, then follow the main road to the gate.

A choice of routes now faces the hiker. You can either go up a ridge north of Meadow Creek almost directly from the parking area, or you can choose a more gradual route up the little valley beyond the ridge. The ridge route gains 1,600 feet elevation in less than a mile and offers good views of Eagle River. The valley route takes nearly 2 miles to gain the same amount of elevation and offers some protection from the wind and a greater sense of having left the city behind. Both trails are simply footpaths worn by hikers and may require a bit of bushwhacking in places.

On foot, for either route, follow the road past the gate. In about 20 yards, the trail to the ridge heads steeply uphill to a radio tower. Turn left on an old road at the tower, but shortly turn off it to the right and follow an obvious trail up the ridge to the summit of what is locally known as "Baldy." Follow the ridge over Baldy onto the broad plateau that leads to Black Tail Rocks.

To find the valley route, follow the road past the gate a little less than a mile. About 100 yards before the end of the road and a cluster of buildings, look for a trail through alder just past a lone spruce tree (you cannot see the buildings at this point). The first few feet of this trail are wet and may require bushwhacking, but the trail breaks out of the alder in about 50 yards and from there is easy to follow. A short distance up the slope, the trail veers left toward the stream. Follow it up the broad valley, toward the pass. The trail leads to a broad plateau (elevation 3,000–3,300 feet).

Follow the south edge of the plateau for ¾ mile to Black Tail Rocks (elevation 4,446 feet). The last part of the climb is fairly steep. From Black Tail Rocks it is a relatively easy traverse along the ridge to Round Top (elevation 4,755 feet) one mile to the north.

Ridge on Round Top, September (Photo: Helen Nienhueser)

Little Peters Creek Access

From Muldoon Road in northeast Anchorage, follow the Glenn Highway 16 miles to the North Birchwood exit and turn right (southbound traffic should cross to the east side of the freeway). In 0.3 mile, turn right onto the Old Glenn Highway. Drive 0.6 mile and turn left onto a gravel road that sweeps uphill 0.1 mile to the trailhead (elevation 450 feet). The turn from the Old Glenn Highway may not be marked. The trail was designed to accommodate snowmobiles in winter and is wide and easy to follow. It twists its way through wooded topography, sometimes steeply up and down, occasionally level. Spruce and birch frame views of Knik Arm, Mt. Susitna, Denali, and other peaks in the Alaska Range. The route splits at one point; the forks rejoin shortly. Overall, the route climbs 1,200 feet in about two miles before cresting a broad ridge near tree line and dropping slightly into the Little Peters Creek valley. There, it intersects the original Ptarmigan Valley Trail.

Follow the old trail up-valley nearly another two miles to tree line and beyond. Once above the trees, pick a route up the slope to your left to Round Top's northwest or west ridge, then follow the ridge to the broad, lichen-covered summit (elevation 4,755 feet).

From Round Top, ambitious hikers can follow the ridge to the southeast to Vista Peak (elevation 5,070 feet). South and slightly west of Round Top are Black Tail Rocks, which can be climbed by following

Round Top's southeast ridge and then veering south and west.

Little Peters Creek is the last water. Look for blueberries in late August.

Both Round Top and Black Tail Rocks can be climbed in winter, but because of avalanche hazard, use ridge approaches to both and avoid gullies (see "Avalanches" in the Introduction). Because the final steep parts may be wind packed, crampons will probably be necessary. The Ptarmigan Valley trail is popular with snowmobilers in winter.

38 THUNDER BIRD FALLS

Round trip: 2 miles
Hiking time: 1 hour
High point: 330 feet
Best: May to October

Total elevation gain: 200 feet in,
130 feet out
USGS map: Anchorage B7 NE

Chugach State Park

A pleasant outing for families with small children, this trail leads through woods to a rushing stream and a view of a pretty waterfall. Although snow patches linger deep in the gorge near the falls well into May, the walk is good any time snow cover permits. Under the birch trees, the forest floor is laced with wild roses and ferns. Along the trail, children can learn to recognize and stay away from devil's club, a prickly, large-leafed shrub up to 6 feet high.

From Anchorage, drive northeast on the Glenn Highway to mile

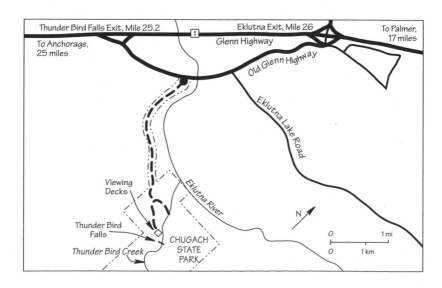

Trail to Thunder Bird Falls, May (Photo: Helen Nienhueser)

25.2, and take the Thunder Bird Falls exit. Drive 0.4 mile to a parking area on the right just before the Eklutna River bridge. The trailhead (elevation 130 feet) is marked. Southbound traffic should exit at Eklutna, mile 26 of the Glenn Highway, cross the bridge over the freeway to the east side, and turn right onto the Old Glenn Highway. Drive 0.6 mile to the trailhead parking area on the left.

An inviting broad trail leads 1 mile to Thunder Bird Creek and the falls. The first part of the trail passes a subdivision. About a half mile from the trailhead, there is a viewing deck looking out over the gorge of Thunder Bird Creek. The view down is impressive and provides an instant understanding of the signs warning hikers to stay away from

Thunder Bird Falls, August (Photo: Marge Maagoe)

the cliffs. Near the end, the trail forks. The right-hand fork becomes a boardwalk that leads to a good view of the falls, hidden in the back of a narrow gorge where the sun reaches only a few hours each day.

The left fork of the trail leads down to the creek. You cannot see the falls when you reach the stream. A trail leads upstream about 100 yards toward them but stops before there is a good view. Do not go beyond the end of the footpath, and do not allow children to explore the cliffs, where they would be in danger of falling. Several deaths have occurred in this manner.

To return to the freeway from the Thunder Bird Falls parking area, turn right as you leave the parking lot, and drive 0.6 mile north on the Old Glenn Highway, crossing the Eklutna River bridge. Follow freeway entrance signs.

The trail is closed to off-road vehicles year-round.

39 EAST TWIN PASS

Round trip: 6½–8 miles
Hiking time: 6–8 hours
High point: 4,450 feet (pass),
  5,050 feet (knob)

Total elevation gain: 3,550 feet
  (pass), 4,150 feet (knob)
Best: July to September
USGS map: Anchorage B6 NW

Chugach State Park

Follow Twin Peaks Trail to timberline and continue up alpine tundra to a magnificent view. Shimmering Eklutna Lake lies southward far below, while to the north spreads the vast panorama of the Mata-

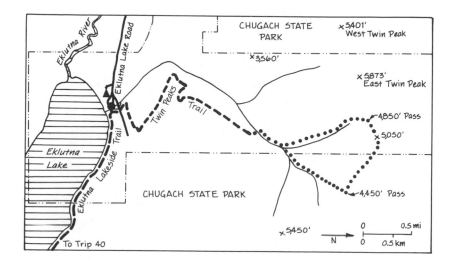

nuska Valley. With the Twin Peaks often in view during the ascent, the hike is mysterious on gray days when clouds swirl around the summits. Chances of seeing Dall sheep are good.

Drive northeast from Anchorage on the Glenn Highway to mile 26, the Eklutna exit. Turn right onto the road coming across the overpass. Southbound traffic should cross the overpass to the east side of the freeway. Turn immediately right onto the frontage road and go 0.4 mile (see map of trip 38). Turn left, following signs for Eklutna Lake. Follow this road about 10 miles to its end at the lake. Drive through the first parking area, to the second parking area and trailhead (elevation 900 feet). Expect to pay a fee for parking.

From the southeast corner of the parking area, walk across a bridge. Turn left on Twin Peaks Trail (marked). Cross a road, following trail signs. The trail then climbs the hill, winding through woods, with occasional views of the lake below.

Brushline, at about 2,700 feet, may be destination enough (2½–3 hours round trip and 1,800 feet elevation gain). A sparkling stream rushes through a small canyon in the alpine bowl beyond the end of the maintained trail; camping or picnicking is tempting.

To continue to the pass, head diagonally down through high grass to

West Twin Peak from access road, August (Photo: Marge Maagoe)

the stream. A path leads from the end of the trail across the first draw coming down from the peak to the northeast. If you lose the path, head for East Twin Pass, the low 4,450-foot pass to the northeast. High grass is soon left behind. Round-trip distance to the pass is about 6½ miles.

For the best Matanuska Valley vistas, follow the ridge crest northwest from the pass to a 5,050-foot knob. To make a circular route, continue west to a second pass at 4,850 feet and then go down the steep south slope, staying west of the stream below this pass.

Climbing either of the peaks requires experience and mountaineering equipment. The usual approach to East Twin is from the 4,850-foot pass.

The trail is closed to off-road vehicles year-round.

40 BOLD PEAK VALLEY

Round trip: 17 miles from parking lot, 7 miles from mile 5 of Lakeside Trail
Hiking time: 0 11 hours from parking lot
Best: late June to early October

High point: 3,700 (moraine), 4,456 feet (ridge)
Total elevation gain: 2,800 or 3,556 feet
USGS map: Anchorage B6

Chugach State Park

The hike to Bold Peak valley, good all summer, is an unsurpassed September outing when Bold Peak is topped with white, the alpine valley is carpeted in red, the lower hillsides are sheathed in gold, and Eklutna Lake shines far below. Watch for moose, marmots, ground squirrels, magpies, Dall sheep, mountain goats, bears, hawks, ptarmigan, and, in season, beautiful wild flowers, high-bush cranberries, and blueberries.

Drive northeast from Anchorage on the Glenn Highway to mile 26, the Eklutna exit. Turn right onto the road coming across the overpass. Southbound traffic should cross the overpass to the east side of the freeway. Turn immediately right onto the frontage road and go 0.4 mile (see map of trip 38). Turn left, following signs for Eklutna Lake. Follow this road about 10 miles to its end at the lake. Drive through the first parking area, to the second parking area and trailhead (elevation 900 feet). Expect to pay a fee for parking.

From the southeast corner of the parking area, walk across a bridge (see map, Trip 39). Turn right and follow Lakeside Trail (an old road) around the lake to mile 5. Cross Bold Creek on a bridge, go 100 feet, and take the left hand trail (marked "Bold Ridge Overlook 3.5 miles"). Bicycles can be ridden to this point in about 30 minutes, substantially reducing the time needed for this hike. A side trail near mile 3 leads to a public use cabin (fee).

Hike the left-hand trail, another old road, as it climbs steeply through deciduous forest to brushline. The old road, in places overgrown with a narrow band of alder, goes another ¾ mile to a knob at about 3,400 feet. The knob is only a little over 2 miles from the lake and may be destination enough. The view is spectacular in all directions.

From the knob, a choice of footpaths beckons the hiker. The easiest leads about a mile along the almost-level valley floor to the glacial moraine at the head of the valley and a superb view of Bold Peak (7,522 feet). Another trail climbs "Bold Ridge" to the south of the knob. On top of the ridge, walk the heights about a mile to point 4456. The views of Bold Peak, Eklutna Lake, Eklutna Glacier, and surrounding mountains are magnificent. The return can be via the same route or by descending the steep, tundra-covered east slope of the ridge to the head of the valley and following the trail on the valley floor back to the knob.

The really energetic can climb the steep scree slope at the head of the valley to Hunter Creek Pass (elevation 4,850 feet), then follow the ridge up to point 5281. There are good views of the relatively inaccessible Hunter Creek valley and the mountain wilderness rising behind it. For a 6-mile loop, follow the northwest ridge from point 5281 back to the lower end of the valley and descend to the knob and the end of the old road. Bold Peak should be attempted only by experienced climbers.

Note that the stream shown on the USGS maps draining the valley is partially underground, limiting access to water. The stream runs on the surface at the head of the valley near the gravel moraine and then goes underground and does not reappear until it is north of point 3465. Good campsites can be found near the stream.

Lakeside Trail, which leads around the lake from Eklutna Lake

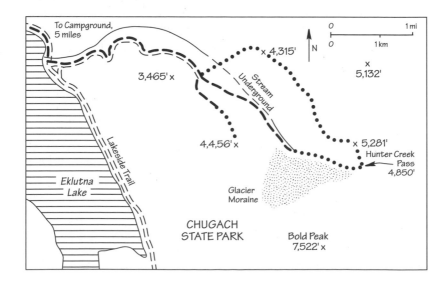

Bold Peak, August (Photo: Helen Nienhueser)

Campground, is 13 miles long and leads to a view of Eklutna Glacier.
It is a good mountain bike trip. Motorized, all-terrain vehicles are permitted, on the road surface only, Sundays through Wednesdays. All
other areas are closed to all-terrain vehicles. Bicyclists can avoid the
motorized vehicles by following a trail that hugs the lakeshore. Its condition is not as good as the main trail but is adequate in most places.

Small powerboats are permitted on Eklutna Lake. There is a walk-
in boat ramp. Contact the Chugach State Park office (address and
phone number in the Appendix) for further information.

41 PIONEER RIDGE

Round trip: 9 miles
Hiking time: 7–10 hours
High point: 5,300 feet

Total elevation gain: 5,100 feet
Best: June to September
USGS maps: Anchorage B6, C6 SE

Matanuska-Susitna Borough and Alaska Division of Land

Pioneer Peak rises 6,400 feet over the Matanuska Valley, its rocky ramparts intimidating even to experienced mountaineers. But try the Knik River–Pioneer Ridge Trail for steep but easy access to the upper reaches of this magnificent peak. From up high, view the expanse of the Knik Glacier and elusive 13,000-foot Mount Marcus Baker, highest of the Chugach Mountains.

From the Muldoon Road–Glenn Highway interchange in Anchorage, drive 25.3 miles to an interchange for the Old Glenn Highway, just

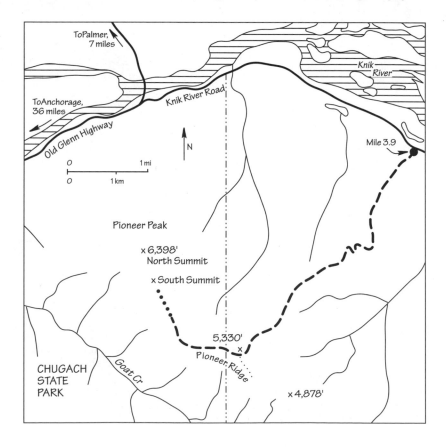

Pioneer Peak from Pioneer Ridge Trail, June (Photo: John Wolfe Jr.)

south of the Knik River bridge. With Pioneer Peak hanging overhead, drive 8.7 miles on the Old Glenn to its intersection with Knik River Road. Find a parking area, marked with a wooden sign for the trailhead, at mile 3.9 of Knik River Road. This trailhead is around the back side of Pioneer, where the intimidating slopes have moderated to merely steep and the peak is not even visible.

The trail starts upward immediately. Within an hour, Knik Glacier and 10,610-foot Mount Goode are visible, the glacier 4 miles wide and more than 25 miles long, the peak sharp and ice-covered. This lower trail can be thick with grass after mid-summer.

Within another half hour, the trail breaks out of the brush and—for a moment—levels off, inviting a rest stop. But save the picnic for higher. Improbably placed, on small flat spots carved by the glacier and surrounded by wildflowers and some of the best views in southcentral Alaska, are two sturdy picnic tables. The first is about 45 minutes above brushline and about halfway to the ridge crest, both in elevation gain and distance. The second is higher, only several hundred vertical feet below the upper trailhead. Either of these makes a fine destination in its own right, with full views of 13,176-foot Marcus Baker, the Knik River, and the Matanuska Valley.

Around 4,300 feet and again around 4,600 feet, the trail angle moderates. At these elevations, approaching the higher picnic table, the route is marked with orange fiberglass stakes but is otherwise not completely obvious because vegetation is sparse. Clouds often swirl in even on fine days, so pay close attention to the stakes and the general lay of the land to aid in finding the route while descending.

Beyond the upper picnic table about 45 minutes, the trail crests the broad back of Pioneer Ridge at 5,300 feet, and suddenly another 180 degrees of view opens up. This view, across Goat Creek valley, is of Bold Peak, Eklutna Glacier and the ice field beyond, and other familiar mountains in Chugach State Park. The ridges above Goat Creek are home to Dall sheep, usually visible in the area. Reaching this goal can easily take 6 hours, but nowhere else in the Chugach does a footpath take hikers so high. For those with energy remaining, the gently rolling ridge top offers easy walking in either direction.

The south summit of Pioneer lies approximately 1½ miles and 1,100 vertical feet northwest of the upper trailhead along the ridge. Although it appears as intimidating as ever, it is accessible with a little rock scrambling to experienced hikers confident in their footing. Sheep trails lead around most rocky promontories, but routefinding is necessary. The south peak is a pleasing summit in its own right, but it is a few feet lower than the north peak. The two peaks are separated by a deep col, and crossing it is recommended only for experienced mountaineers equipped with ropes.

42 LAZY MOUNTAIN AND McROBERTS CREEK

Round trip: 5–7 miles
Hiking time: 5–6 hours
High point: Lazy Mountain 3,720 feet

Total elevation gain: 3,120 feet
Best: May to October
USGS map: Anchorage C6

Matanuska-Susitna Borough and Alaska Division of Land

Lazy Mountain is a steep hike with a nice summit to let hikers know they are finished. The Matanuska Peak Trail in the adjacent McRoberts Creek valley is somewhat easier but has a less distinct hiking goal. These primitive trails, with variations on the same fine views, are close enough to connect, and a loop trip is possible. Looming beyond both is Matanuska Peak, a summit for the truly hardy.

The trails are suitable for children, although kids will take more time. The views are principally of the Matanuska Valley farming district, the silver waters of Cook Inlet, and Pioneer Peak jutting above the Knik River. The lower portions of both trails wind through tall grass, which, even on a clear day, may be wet with dew, so take a pair of rain pants. Wildflowers abound; new species of flowers introduce themselves with every hundred feet of elevation gained, culminating on the Lazy Mountain ridge crest and at the upper end of McRoberts Creek in minute lichens, with brilliant pinhead-sized sporangia, clinging to the rocks. Three hike variations and the Matanuska Peak climbing routes are described here.

Lazy Mountain

To reach the Lazy Mountain trailhead, drive to mile 42.1 of the Glenn Highway (36 miles northeast of Anchorage at a stoplight near Palmer). Turn east onto West Arctic Avenue, easily identified by a Tesoro gas station on the corner. Follow this road, which becomes the Old Glenn Highway, 2.3 miles through Palmer and across the Matanuska River to Clark–Wolverine Road (marked). Turn left, continue 0.7 mile to a T junction, and then turn right onto Huntley Road (marked). Drive 1 mile to the crest of a hill and a Y intersection. Go right and downhill 0.2 mile to a parking area (elevation 600 feet).

The 2½-mile trail begins at the left (northeast) side of the parking area across a culvert. A level, wider, gravel trail that starts between large boulders, the Morgan Horse Trail, leads to Matanuska Peak Trail, nearly 1¼ miles or about 35 minutes away.

Start up Lazy Mountain Trail. Don't be confused by an indistinct fork in the path a dozen yards up the trail; go right on the more distinct right-hand trail. It is well defined all the way to brushline.

The path becomes quite steep and is muddy and slippery when wet. Beyond the first of several false summits, where the growth gives way to low berry bushes, the grade becomes more gentle. From here pick your own route up the tundra-covered slopes. The last 200 feet of the summit ridge of Lazy Mountain are narrow and exposed; children will need help. Carry drinking water.

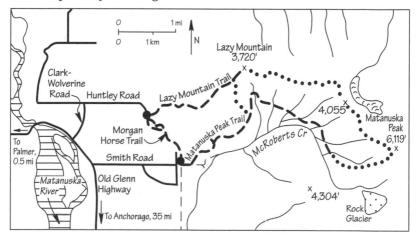

149

*View of Pioneer Peak and Twin Peaks from Lazy Mountain, June
(Photo: Helen Nienhueser)*

McRoberts Creek Valley

To reach the McRoberts Creek valley, start in Palmer as described
in the first paragraph of the preceding Lazy Mountain directions, but
bypass Clark-Wolverine Road and proceed 0.4 mile from the Clark-
Wolverine intersection to an intersection with Smith Road (marked).
Turn east (uphill) on Smith Road, and continue 1.4 miles until the road
ends at a T intersection with Harmony Avenue. Park off the road (elevation 525 feet); space is tight. The trail, which starts as a vehicle
track, is marked Matanuska Peak Trail. It heads east toward the

mountains off the end of Smith Road. Within a couple of minutes, the Morgan Horse trail crosses at right angles. The trail to the left connects with the Lazy Mountain trailhead 30-40 minutes away. Parking there and hiking the Morgan Horse Trail to this intersection is an alternative.

To continue up McRoberts Creek, hike about 15 minutes on the main route to the top of a long, straight, steep hill and an iron gate. Just past the gate, an ATV trail heads uphill on the left. It forks immediately. Take the right fork up a root-covered footpath. This is the Matanuska Peak Trail, which leads to the upper McRoberts Creek valley. A couple of minor routes join or diverge; bear right and uphill to treeline. At brushline, the path dips through a deep ravine. Beyond the ravine, the path underfoot eventually becomes somewhat less obvious, but the route is well marked with orange fiberglass stakes to the head of the valley. This upper section between miles 2 and 4 has only gentle grades. A reasonable end point for a hike, unless you wish to climb Matanuska Peak, is in the upper valley where the route begins to steepen again.

Lazy Mountain–McRoberts Creek Loop

To make a 7-mile loop trip, start up the McRoberts route. As the trail heads into the ravine at brushline, diverge to the left, and head cross-country uphill over tundra. It is about 1,000 vertical feet and ⅔ mile to Lazy Mountain Trail. Reaching it, continue another several hundred vertical feet to the top of Lazy Mountain. Then descend Lazy Mountain Trail, and return to the McRoberts trailhead on the connecting path described earlier. There are several small loops near the north end of this connecting trail. All paths ultimately lead to the same place, but the quickest is probably the lowest trail.

Matanuska Peak

Those with boundless energy may want to continue from either trailhead to Matanuska Peak (6,119 feet), the real mountain, looming at the head of McRoberts Creek and 4 miles along the undulating ridge to the east of Lazy Mountain. The hike is a long one—10–14 hours round trip from either trailhead. From Lazy Mountain, follow the ridge crest, and head to the right up the northwest ridge of Matanuska Peak. From the top of this ridge, approach the summit rock pile up a loose scree slope. Go right at the final rocks. A rope belay is not necessary if the route is carefully chosen.

The McRoberts route to the summit is shorter (11 miles round trip instead of 13), although the last 2,000 feet are very steep and include a stretch of loose talus (blocks of rock) that could be dangerous. Orange route markers continue from the end of the trail to near the summit. Because of the length of either summit route, consider taking flashlights on all but the longest days of summer. The summit usually has snow until July.

43 REED LAKES

**Round trip: Lower Reed Lake 7
miles, Upper Reed Lake 9 miles
Hiking time: 5–7 hours
High point: 4,250 feet**

**Total elevation gain: 1,850 feet
Best: July to September
USGS map: Anchorage D6**

*Alaska Division of Parks and Outdoor Recreation and Alaska Division
of Land*

At the foot of towering granite spires reminiscent of the high Sierra,
plunging cascades feed alpine Reed Lakes. On the edge of the vast wilderness of the Talkeetna Mountains, this mountain world is unlike any
other near Anchorage. Watch for ptarmigan, marmots, ground squirrels, pikas, northern shrikes, and golden eagles.

Reach the trailhead from mile 49.5 of the Glenn Highway by turning
west on a road marked "Fishhook Road." (This road is also known as
Palmer–Fishhook and Fishhook–Willow Road.) This paved road begins
1.5 miles beyond Palmer's West Arctic Avenue (the farthest north
Palmer stoplight). It becomes the gravel Hatcher Pass road. Follow it
to elevations above treeline. About 14 miles from Glenn Highway, it
rounds a sharp switchback at the Motherlode Lodge. Proceed another
0.9 mile to Archangel Road (marked), which begins with a sharp
switchback to the right off the Hatcher Pass road. Drive 2.3 miles on
this unmaintained road to a pullout on the right, well marked as the
Reed Lakes trailhead (elevation 2,400 feet).

To reach Reed Lakes, walk or bike the eroded Snowbird Mine road
about 1½ miles to its end at an ill-kept cabin (elevation 2,700 feet).
This is at the site of the old Snowbird Mine village; the shack is ru-
mored to have been the village blacksmith shop. Building foundations
and other scraps of history are buried in the brush near this cabin. The
mine itself was high on the mountainside to the northwest up Glacier

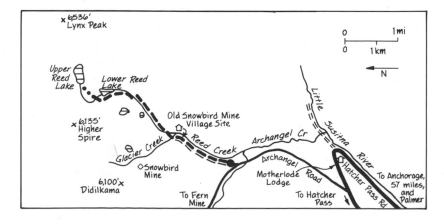

Creek. From this point, Lower Reed Lake is 2 miles away, and Upper Reed Lake is a mile farther.

Reed Creek valley is not obvious from the cabin. The creek comes down from the middle valley north of the cabin; look for cascades part way up it. From the cabin, follow a footpath to the first stream, Glacier Creek, and cross it on a bridge. About 100 feet farther, cross Reed Creek on a second bridge.

Reed Creek valley, August (Photo: John Wolfe Jr.)

After crossing Reed Creek, the trail climbs steeply uphill and is becoming eroded by the passage of many feet. Please stay on the main trail and avoid cutting corners on the few switchbacks that do exist to help reduce further problems. The trail contours left below the hilltop to an area covered by large granite boulders. Boulder-hopping is necessary here, a difficult task for less-experienced hikers, young children, and dogs. Beyond the boulder field, follow sparkling Reed Creek through grassy meadows and past small clear pools that reflect the surrounding mountains. Cross to the north side of the creek at these pools, and climb 200 feet to the aqua beauty that is Lower Reed Lake (elevation 3,750 feet). Stay high on the left above the stream. Beyond the lake, a lovely waterfall cascades over rock slabs.

To reach Upper Reed Lake (elevation 4,250 feet), a mile from the lower lake, skirt around the falls to the left, crossing rocks and grassy meadows. Beyond a shallow pond, vivid Upper Reed Lake appears. It is larger than the lower lake and set in a cirque at the base of Lynx Peak (elevation 6,536 feet). Granite spires and sheer faces rise high above talus and glaciers. The lakes are often ice-covered into July, and ice forms again by mid-September.

Many good campsites are available, from just beyond the boulder field to the mossy hummocks at Upper Reed Lake. No firewood is available in this alpine area; bring a stove for cooking. Hardy types swim in these chilly waters on hot days.

The ill-kept cabin in Snowbird valley is open for public shelter, but it needs straightening. Leave it a little better than you find it, and it may eventually become useful. From the cabin, the hanging valley of Glacier Creek makes a nice alternate hike and leads to Snowbird Glacier. The trip from the Hatcher Pass road to the Snowbird Mine cabin is a good winter ski or snowshoe tour over gently sloping terrain. Park in a plowed turnout near the beginning of Archangel Road, and take a shovel in case your car gets stuck. Snowmobiles use Archangel Road and the area west of the road but are prohibited on the east (Reed Lakes) side of the road. Contact the Alaska Division of Parks Mat-Su office for more information (see the Appendix).

44 HATCHER PASS SKI TOUR

One way: 14 miles
Skiing time: 5–8 hours
High point: 3,886 feet

Total elevation gain: 950 feet
Best: December to April
USGS maps: Anchorage D7, D8

Alaska Division of Parks and Outdoor Recreation and Alaska Division of Land

The unplowed portion of the Hatcher Pass road provides a beautiful ski tour through the Talkeetna Mountains. While the Hatcher Pass area is perhaps most popular for backcountry telemark skiing, this trip

En route to Hatcher Pass, November

is perfect for those who don't telemark but still love a long ski in the mountains.

A short 1½-mile climb with an elevation gain of 950 feet places the skier at Hatcher Pass. From there it is all downhill for 12½ miles, an elevation loss of about 2,300 feet. For those wishing to combine touring and telemarking, there are good areas for carving turns on the descent.

A potential flaw in this rosy picture is the 2-hour drive between the ends of the route. Arrange to be picked up at the Willow end of the trail, if possible, or plan to join the Nordic Skiing Association of Anchorage (address in the Appendix) on its annual tour and be picked up by bus.

While the main route generally follows the road, the mountain slopes and nearby valleys garbed in winter finery invite exploration. But be wary of avalanches. Snowmobilers also use this area.

To reach the trailhead, drive to mile 49.5 of the Glenn Highway (1.5 miles north of the West Arctic Avenue stoplight on the northern edge of Palmer). Turn west onto a road marked "Fishhook Road." (This is also known as Palmer–Fishhook Road and Fishhook–Willow Road; see the area map for the North of Anchorage region.) This becomes the Hatcher Pass road. Drive 14 miles, passing through the scenic gorge of the Little Susitna River, to a sharp switchback at Motherlode Lodge. The road is steep, narrow, and winding. Although it is generally well maintained, cars should be equipped with studded winter tires or four-

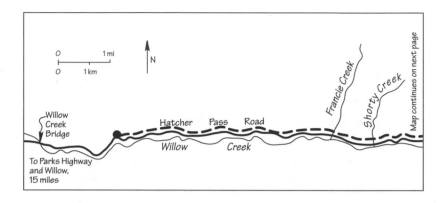

wheel drive; chains may be necessary. At the A-frames of Hatcher Pass Lodge, 3.5 miles beyond the switchback, park in an area provided.

Ski a couple hundred yards back alongside (but not on) the roadway you just drove up. The road to the pass itself is unplowed; ski up it. Snowmobiles generally pack the snow up to the pass but use the west side less. The pass is where the long downhill begins. Finding the route is no problem, as the drainage pattern is definite and leads naturally along Willow Creek and the road, which is usually not plowed. Ski the road, or ski anywhere in the valley, taking care only to stay away from the bases of steep avalanche-prone slopes. Note the old mine buildings high on the slopes to the right near Craigie Creek.

From the Willow end, the road is plowed at least 17 miles, to about 2 miles east of the Willow Creek bridge. The plowed parking area at the Willow Creek bridge makes a good destination, although some may prefer to ski the remaining distance to Willow. Alaska Railroad trains pass through Willow on a limited winter schedule, giving the skier the option of returning to Anchorage on the train. Check with the railroad office (address and phone number in the Appendix) for a schedule and pickup point.

The Hatcher Pass area also has a variety of short day trips available to those who don't have time to complete the full tour. Spend a pleasant afternoon touring in the broad and gently sloping area between the A-frames and the buildings of Independence Mine State Historic Park. The mine buildings and the Gold Cord Bowl above and behind them make a good place for ski explorations. Hatcher Pass Lodge grooms ski trails and asks for a fee from those using the set tracks. A popular destination for backcountry telemark skiers is Microdot Ridge, across the valley from Independence Mine and usually accessed from the A-frames. Another popular spot is April Bowl, which sits on the mountain to the left (south) of Hatcher Pass proper. Most slopes in the area have been skied, but many gullies are steep enough to avalanche. Only those trained and equipped for avalanche avoidance and rescue should attempt steep slopes (see "Avalanches" in the Introduction).

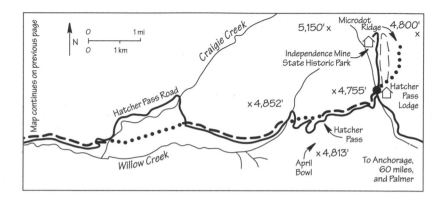

The weather in Hatcher Pass often can be still and warm, but it is unpredictable. Wind gusts can create ground blizzards on the clearest of days. Temperatures are generally colder than in Anchorage. Take extra warm clothes and a flashlight with strong batteries. In midwinter, daylight lasts only from 9:30 A.M. to 4 P.M.

To reach the Willow end of the trail from the Independence Mine area, drive 10½ miles back down the Hatcher Pass road toward Palmer. Turn right onto Wasilla–Fishhook Road, the second road to the right after leaving the mountains, marked "Wasilla 11 [miles]." At Wasilla, turn right onto the Parks Highway, and drive 29 miles to mile 71.2, the junction with the west end of the Hatcher Pass road (or Fishhook–Willow Road). Turn right and drive about 17 miles to a parking area at the Willow Creek bridge, near the end of the plowed road. To reach Willow from Anchorage (71 miles), drive the Glenn Highway 35 miles to the Parks Highway; follow the Parks Highway to Willow.

45 CRAIGIE CREEK

Round trip: 3–9 miles   **Total elevation gain: 950 feet**
Hiking time: 2–7 hours   **Best: late July to early October**
High point: 4,250 feet   **USGS map: Anchorage D7**

Alaska Division of Land

Take a picnic lunch to a blue-green alpine lake at the base of precipitous peaks and spires. The short walk is just right for families with children, but don't overlook this charming hike to Dogsled Pass as an entrance to outstanding wilderness hiking deep into the Talkeetna Mountains.

To reach Craigie Creek, drive to mile 49.5 of the Glenn Highway (43.5 miles northeast of Anchorage and 1.5 miles north of Palmer's

157

West Arctic Avenue stoplight), and turn west onto a road marked
"Fishhook Road." (This is also known as Palmer–Fishhook Road and
Fishhook–Willow Road; see area map for the North of Anchorage section.) Fishhook Road becomes the gravel Hatcher Pass road, a narrow,
steep, and winding route unsafe for trailers and large campers. Drive
about 18.8 miles from the Glenn Highway, through the scenic gorge of
the Little Susitna River and past the side road to Independence Mine
State Historic Park, to the crest of Hatcher Pass. About 1.4 miles beyond (west of) the pass, the road forks; take the left fork. Continue another 3.2 miles to a side road that turns right into the valley of Craigie
Creek and may be marked "Craigie Creek Trail." The total distance
from Glenn Highway to this point is 23.4 miles.

Craigie Creek Trail is a very narrow, very rocky, unmaintained old
road. It is passable for about 3 miles by vehicles with good clearance
and four-wheel drive. The first mile or so is extraordinarily rough.
Nearly level and lined with wildflowers, it makes a great hike and presents mountain bikers with some good technical challenges (rocks).
Note that walking it makes the entire hike about 9 miles instead of 3
miles round trip.

Because of deep snow, the road over Hatcher Pass is virtually never
open before the third week in June. Craigie Creek Trail should be free
of snow by then but may have wet and soft spots. Those who drive
should park well off the road. One possible parking spot (elevation
3,300 feet) is on the right where the ruins of a cabin are visible across
the creek, about 2.8 miles from the main road.

At the beginning of Craigie Creek Trail, note the adit entrances of
Lucky Shot and War Baby mines high on the mountains to the left.
Gold mining in the Craigie Creek area began prior to 1919 and continued at least through 1930. On-again, off-again mining activity has
taken place in recent years. If areas are posted against trespassing, respect the signs. The route may cross private property, although hikers
have used this access for years without complications. In any case, do
not disturb buildings or equipment, and leave rocks or other minerals
where they lie.

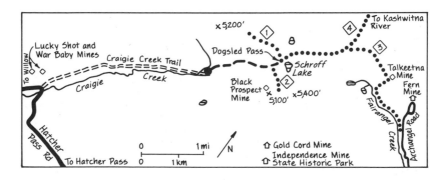

Schroff Lake, Dogsled Pass, July (Photo: Susan Olsen)

From the possible parking areas up this old road, continue on foot as the track climbs gently, passing old buildings and waterfalls. The road then becomes a foot trail leading high above timberline to Dogsled Pass (elevation 4,250 feet) and a lovely tarn locally known as Schroff Lake. The north side of the pass is covered by acres of granite boulders, and campsites near the pass and lake are hard to find.

Hikes and climbs abound. Several possibilities are outlined here. Numbers are keyed to the map:

(1) From Dogsled Pass, an easy walk leads up the west ridge to several high points.

(2) A rock scramble up the gully to the southeast next to the old Black Prospect Mine entrance leads to a ridge crest and a view of the historic Independence Mine buildings far below.

(3) From Dogsled Pass, a second pass to the right (northeast) across the flats leads to a high valley containing the Talkeetna Mine. Descend to Fairangel Creek and follow it to Archangel Road (see trip 43).

(4) A vast area of alpine lakes and 6,000-foot peaks north of Dogsled Pass offers several days of hiking to the Kashwitna River drainage.

This area is also accessible from Willow on the Parks Highway at mile 71.2. In winter the Hatcher Pass road is not plowed between Hatcher Pass Lodge (Independence Mine area) and the Willow Creek bridge, about 17 miles from the Parks Highway.

46 NANCY LAKE CANOE TRAILS

Lynx Lake Loop: 8 miles
Allow 7 hours to 2 days
Best: late May to early October

USGS map: Tyonek C1; for Little
Susitna River, Anchorage C8

Nancy Lake State Recreation Area

The Nancy Lake State Recreation Area offers a lovely, tranquil, popular canoe trip, Lynx Lake Loop, through a chain of fourteen forest-rimmed lakes. Loons dot the lakes, bears occasionally use the portages, and fishing is good in several of the lakes. The twelve overland portages are on good trails and are well marked.

Take the Parks Highway to mile 67.3 (from Anchorage). Turn west onto Nancy Lake Parkway, a wide gravel road that may resemble a rough washboard. Drive 4.7 miles to the canoe trailhead at Tanaina Lake.

Pick up a "Summer Guide to Nancy Lake State Recreation Area" at the trailhead if not before. The map is very helpful in finding the portages. The loop can be taken in either direction, but going by way of Milo Pond, in a counterclockwise direction, puts the longest portages at the beginning of the trip. Begin the trip by paddling to the south end of Tanaina Lake and portaging to Milo *Pond*. Note that the first lake in the opposite direction is named Milo *Lake*.

All of the portages are under a half mile, and most are considerably shorter. Some have boardwalks over wet spots. Several require carrying the canoe uphill. The portage between Frazer and Jackknife lakes is by water.

The best camping is at the designated campsites between Little Noluck and Big Noluck lakes (a little over an hour from the trailhead), on Lynx Lake (a little over 4 hours from the trailhead via Milo Pond and a little over 2 hours via Milo Lake), and at either end of Ardaw Lake (about an hour from the trailhead). Each of these campsite areas has an outhouse. There are also four public-use cabins on Lynx Lake Loop, one at James Lake, and three on Lynx Lake. The James Lake log cabin is the nicest. Make reservations to rent a cabin with Alaska State Parks Mat-Su Area office or with the Department of Natural Resources Public Information Center (addresses in the Appendix).

All of the lakes except Lynx are completely surrounded by public land. Lynx has some private land and private cabins around it, and camping is permitted only at the designated campsites. Airplanes and boats with outboard motors are allowed on Lynx Lake, but not on the other lakes.

Several variations on the standard loop trip are possible. An extension is to head south from Lynx Lake to Butterfly and Skeetna lakes, then return via the same route. There are several campsites on Skeetna Lake, and Butterfly Lake has good fishing. It is also possible to enter the canoe system via the Little Susitna River. Access is from mile 57 on Parks Highway. It takes 4–5 hours on the river to reach the portage for Skeetna Lake (marked). The river portion requires more canoeing experience than do the lakes.

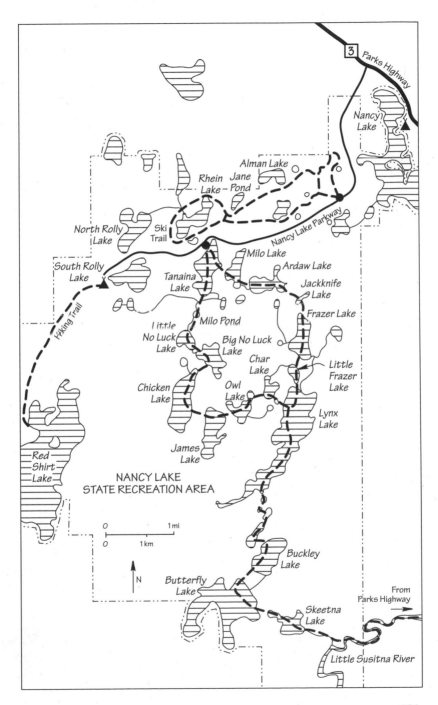

Bring binoculars for watching birds and spotting portages. Rubber boots will keep feet dry, and a head net is nice to have for the portages. Canoes can be rented nearby and may be available at the trailhead (addresses in the Appendix).

Nancy Lake Recreation Area also offers four public-use cabins on Nancy Lake and four on Red Shirt Lake. All can be reached by skiing, snowmobiling, or flying. The Nancy Lake cabins can be reached by boat and three of the four can be reached by hiking. The cabins on Red Shirt Lake can be reached by a 3-mile hiking trail and renting a canoe. (One can be reached without a canoe, but there is no trail.) Firewood and drinking water are not provided at any of the cabins, but all have wood stoves.

In winter 10 miles of maintained cross-country ski trails loop through the rolling, lake-dotted country north of Nancy Lake Parkway. The winter trailhead is at mile 2.2 of the Parkway and the Nancy Lake public-use cabins are only about a mile away in the opposite direction. When the lakes freeze solid before the snow falls, the lakes also offer the opportunity for overnight ice-skating trips. Take a light plastic sled for gear, and reserve a cabin for a novel weekend. Take warm boots for the "portages."

Chicken Lake, June (Photo: Helen Nienhueser)

47 PETERS HILLS

Round trip: 4–14 miles
Allow 3 hours to 2 days
High point: 2,840 or 3,929 feet

Total elevation gain: 1,000–2,480 feet
Best: July to September
USGS map: Talkeetna C2

Denali State Park

The majestic white presence of Denali (Mount McKinley) dominates the skyline 40 miles north of the Peters Hills. While the view from point 2840, 2 miles from the trailhead, is excellent, the vista up the Tokositna Glacier from Long Point at the eastern end of the ridge is breathtaking. Famed Alaska artist Sydney Laurence painted many of his canvases of Denali from just below Long Point.

Excellent camping beside small alpine lakes makes this a good backpacking trip for families with children. Look for blueberries and lingonberries in season, and watch for grizzly (brown) bears. The hike is particularly scenic in early September when the rich reds and golds of autumn foliage are at their best. But note that the area is also popular with hunters beginning in late August, particularly on weekends.

A few cautions: the trip described here is a cross country hike, much of it without any trail. The first part follows an all-terrain-vehicle trail through brush. The footpath that branches off the ATV trail peters out and eventually disappears entirely. You are on your own to find the best route. There is no developed trailhead, there is no trail maintenance, and there are no signs. Finding the point where the ATV trail leaves the road can be a challenge. Some off-trail experience is necessary to ensure that you can find your way back to your car. A map and compass and the ability to use them are desirable in the event the clouds settle down on these hills, as they often do. The last 12½ miles of driving are rough.

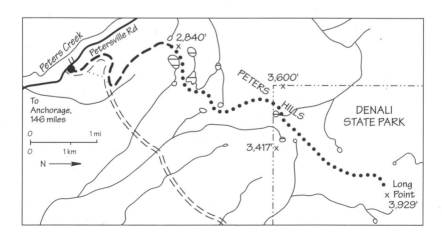

Denali (Mount McKinley) from Peters Hills, September

At mile 114.8 of the Parks Highway (115 miles north of Anchorage), turn west onto Petersville Road at the tiny town of Trapper Creek. The Peters Hills are 31 miles away. As far as Peters Creek and the Forks Roadhouse (18.4 miles), the road is fairly good gravel. Bear right at the roadhouse. From this point the road narrows, is poorly maintained, and may have deep mud holes during spring breakup. When the road is dry, usually by July, cars with normal clearance should have little trouble reaching the trail, although a few eroded sections may challenge driving skills. Allow at least 4 hours to drive the 146 miles from Anchorage. Contact the Alaska Department of Transportation for a road condition report (phone number in the Appendix).

North of the Forks Roadhouse 11.9 miles, in the bottom of a small valley, watch for the buildings of the Petersville placer mine. To reach the trail, drive exactly 1 mile farther and find a gravelly all-terrain vehicle trail leaving the right side of the road (don't be confused by a muddier track leaving the road 0.8 mile beyond the mine buildings). Park just a few yards beyond the trailhead in a open gravel area below the main road to the left (elevation 1,825 feet).

The first viewpoint is 2 miles away. Follow the trail uphill. It bends to the left and follows the dry crest of a low ridge, then makes a broad U-turn to the right and traverses a hillside. This arc makes an end run around a small drainage and is pleasant walking. As an option, a muddy shortcut crosses the drainage and eliminates a little distance.

Beyond the arc, the trail climbs a short hill, levels, and heads northeast. It then descends slightly to a creek. About 50 feet before the creek, find a narrow footpath departing to the left and heading toward a prominent triangular high point to the left (northwest). Pass below and to the right of this triangular point, and continue on the trail toward point 2840 until the path becomes intermittent. Proceed cross-country when necessary, and go to the top of point 2840 for a fine view. Go past it to reach Long Point (elevation 3,929 feet), 5 miles away.

To reach Long Point via the least brushy route, weave through the lakes and high points along the ridge as shown on the map. From the outlet of the lake east of point 2840, head northeast, and contour around the eastern end of the heart-shaped lake on a dry, low ridge. Cross the brushy valley between two tiny lakes. Then climb toward point 3600, following dry-looking, brownish patches on its south ridge. Whether you go to the top or contour to the right (at about 3,400 feet), the rest of the route to Long Point is a gently rising 2-mile walk.

Follow this tundra-covered ridge as far as time permits. Sunlight, clouds, and storms sweeping through the mountain panorama to the north are hypnotic. Watch the sunset, the sunrise, and the northern lights play with the continent's highest peak and its consorts. Camp anywhere. Water is easily available, but take a stove for cooking. Take a USGS topographic map and compass, too, because when clouds roll in across the hilltops, it can be difficult to find the trail for descent. The eastern half of the ridge lies in Denali State Park.

Monarch Peak in the Talkeetna Mountains, trip 48 (Photo: Helen Nienhueser)

CHICKALOON TO VALDEZ

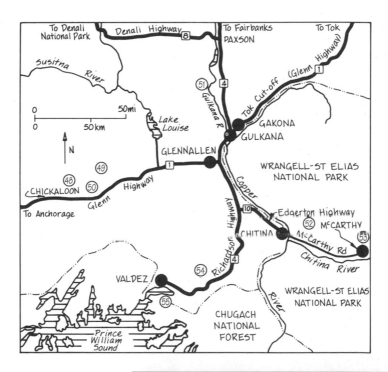

Arctic ground squirrel

48 HICKS CREEK–CHITNA PASS

One way: 42 miles
Allow 4–5 days
High point: 4,700 feet
Best: late June to September

Total elevation gain: 4,120 feet
eastbound, 3,680 feet westbound
USGS maps: Anchorage D2, D3, D4

Alaska Division of Land and U.S. Bureau of Land Management

The Talkeetna Mountains, which invite endless wandering, are a fascinating wilderness of peaks, tundra, alpine valleys, and clear mountain streams, most it far from civilization. The trip over Chitna Pass is nearly circular and includes some unmaintained trails. Using the trails as access and topographic maps as a guide, many other trips are possible, limited primarily by time and food supply.

According to old-timers, prospectors traveled parts of this trail in the early 1900s. The route took them from Knik (which was accessible by boat from Seattle in the summer) and Chickaloon, up Boulder

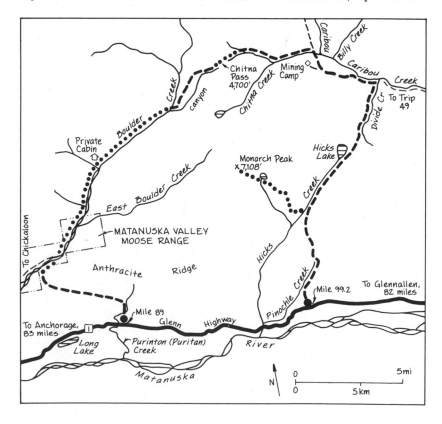

Creek, over Chitna Pass, and along Caribou Creek to Alfred Creek (see trip 49). Their destinations were gold prospects and mines on Alfred and Albert creeks. Today, many of these routes are all-terrain vehicle (ATV) trails, still used by miners and by hunters in the fall.

The route described here is on unmarked, unmaintained ATV, horse, and game trails—and for short stretches it is without trails. The trip is not for novices; it is possible to become confused about the route and become lost. A 1:63,360 scale USGS map is essential; help is far away. Do not go alone, and do not go unless the party includes expert map readers. Experienced backpackers in good condition and able to follow USGS maps will find that these routes lead to delightful country, if they don't mind using ATV trails. Watch for caribou, moose, black bears, grizzly (brown) bears, Dall sheep, wolves, and coyotes.

To reach the trail, take the Glenn Highway to mile 99.2 (from Anchorage). Park opposite the trailhead near powerline pole 7746 in an area defined by boulders (elevation 1,776 feet), or turn north onto a dirt road and park without blocking the road. Construction of the new highway will require driving to about mile 100, turning north onto the old Glenn, and then driving to the mile 99.2 trailhead. This first section of trail is known locally as Pinochle Creek or Hicks Creek Trail.

On foot, follow the dirt road north. It quickly becomes an ATV trail that climbs above timberline to a 3,150-foot pass visible in the distance. The trail over the pass is good, although the lower ground on either side of the pass is rutted and often mucky. The north side of the pass is especially wet, and both sides are worse for the wear of tracked vehicles, but the total trip is worth persevering for.

Not far beyond the pass, the trail descends steeply to Hicks Creek, at 3,000 feet. A side trip from the creek heads northwest to a small alpine lake (5,000 feet) about 5 miles away, where there is good camping but no firewood. Use a USGS map to find your way there. Monarch Peak (7,108 feet), towering above the lake, is the highest in the area and is a steep but easy climb.

The main trail continues to Hicks Lake. The trail may vary somewhat from year to year. Pick whichever side of the creek looks easiest. Camping is possible near the south end of the lake. Watch for muskrats in the water. Beyond Hicks Lake, the ATV trail becomes drier and pleasant. It crosses an indistinct 3,300-foot pass, then follows Divide Creek down to Caribou Creek at 2,800 feet elevation, about 4 miles from Hicks Lake.

Follow the trail up the south side of Caribou Creek, passing good campsites. Beyond the creek junction 1½–2 miles, follow the most distinct route as it climbs the bank to avoid cliffs and winds along higher ground roughly paralleling the creek (another track continues up the creek bank). Beyond a small ravine and upstream of the junction of Chitna and Caribou creeks, the trail forks. The right branch leads steeply down to Chitna Creek. The left fork climbs a hill to a mining camp. Descend to the creek.

Wade across Chitna Creek. It is swift but usually not deep or difficult to cross. The trail up the opposite bank goes up two distinct levels.

Follow it to the top of the second bluff. The ATV trail then continues north along Caribou Creek. *Do not follow it,* unless you are purposefully diverging from the route described here. Instead, search to the left and pick up a narrow footpath that winds along the edge of the bluff, following the Chitna Creek valley upstream.

The trail blends with game trails, but it does continue nearly to Chitna Pass and is worth staying on. About 2½ miles from Caribou Creek, turn northwest up a tributary of Chitna Creek toward Chitna Pass. Map-reading skills are essential to find this drainage that leads to the pass, because the trail disappears here for a while. Two separate creek channels come down this one valley, but only the larger ravine farther to the west shows as a creek on the USGS map. You may not find much water in the smaller ravine, but it is an indication that this is the correct valley to ascend. Make your way uphill between these two channels, and rediscover the trail.

At 3,600 feet the vegetation changes from brush to open tundra. A gradual climb to Chitna Pass (elevation 4,700 feet), about 2½ miles away, traverses fine country for camping and exploring. The trail mostly vanishes. Nearby 6,000-foot peaks can be easily climbed. Water is available, but firewood is not.

Southwest of Chitna Pass, the route parallels a small creek, and a well-defined footpath reappears. Follow it to nearly level ground and a bend to the left. A short time later, about 2½ miles from the pass, the stream plunges into a small canyon. At that point, the trail leaves the creek, traverses out to the right, and descends the ridge all the way down to Boulder Creek. It does not drop steeply to Boulder Creek directly west of Chitna Pass as shown on the USGS map. The views of the Boulder Creek valley from the ridge crest make the whole trip worthwhile.

About 4 miles from Chitna Pass the well-defined trail ends when it enters the Boulder Creek gravel bars. If the water level is low enough, walking the riverbed, splashing across the braided channels, is by far the easiest mode of travel. At higher water, cross Boulder Creek once and stay on the northwest side where occasional stretches of trail alternate with occasional stretches of bushwhacking. Following the southeast riverbank requires scrambling over bluffs, necessary perhaps if Boulder Creek is in flood and cannot be easily crossed. Camping is good on the riverbars.

From where the trail enters the gravel bars, it is more than 10 miles down Boulder Creek to Anthracite Ridge. The crest of Anthracite Ridge drops steeply to the riverbank. Find the Purinton Creek Trail on the east bank of Boulder Creek right at the base of the ridge. On some maps it may be labeled the Chickaloon–Knik–Nelchina Trail. Follow this trail south, then east to the Glenn Highway. This rolling trail has some boggy spots, but generally the walking is good. On a clear day, the approach to the Purinton Creek trailhead is spectacular with its panoramic view to the south of the rugged Chugach Mountains.

To reach the Purinton Creek trailhead by road, drive to mile 89 of

Near Chitna Pass, August

the Glenn Highway. Parking is available in a pullout by the Purinton Creek bridge (elevation 2,100 feet). About 75 yards east of Purinton Creek is a dirt road that starts northward and bends immediately to the east. Respect private property along the road. Soon, it bends north again and ascends a very steep hill. A new trailhead at mile 90.7 avoids private property but is more suitable for ATVs than hikers.

The two ends of the trail are reasonable for day trips by mountain bike in dry weather, although each has a long steep hill that will require a tough stint of pushing the bike. Hicks Creek valley is too wet for cycling. The Purinton Creek Trail is hilly. Much more of the route can be used for ski touring, either for day trips from either trailhead or as a several-day trip for experienced ski tourers and winter campers. The route near the trailheads is likely to be packed by snowmobiles. In midwinter prepare for very cold weather as temperatures to minus thirty degrees Fahrenheit are not uncommon.

49 SYNCLINE MOUNTAIN

Circuit 26 miles, traverse 24 miles
Allow 3 days
High point: circuit 4,350 feet,
  traverse 5,471 feet

Total elevation gain: circuit 2,200
  feet, traverse 4,400 feet
Best: June to September
USGS maps: Anchorage D1, D2

Alaska Division of Land and U.S. Bureau of Land Management

A network of trails around Syncline Mountain provides access into the backcountry of the Talkeetna Mountains, inhabited primarily by caribou, sheep, miners, and—during the last part of summer—hunters. Two different trips are possible, a circumnavigation of Syncline Mountain and a traverse over it. Each has a possible variation or two. On either trip watch for caribou, sheep, ptarmigan, ground squirrels, snowshoe hares, porcupines, water ouzels, hawks, moose, black bears, grizzlies, coyotes, and wolves. In season there are blueberries and the gamut of Alaska wildflowers. Both trips are rugged and require routefinding skills and backcountry experience. This description first introduces the routes and then gives specific details on each.

The circuit of the mountain follows the valleys of Squaw, Caribou, Alfred, and Pass creeks and then climbs over Belanger Pass to complete the loop. The route follows all-terrain-vehicle (ATV) trails and mining roads most of the way, but in places hikers must search for game trails.

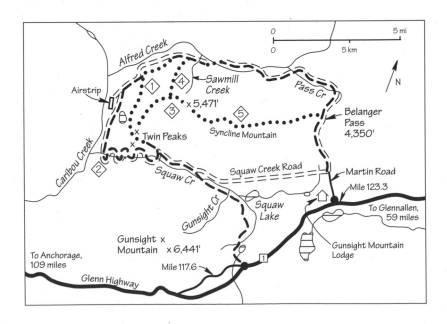

The traverse over the mountain is steep but not difficult. It offers nice views of the Chugach and Talkeetna mountains and avoids most of the mining areas. Hikers are more likely to see sheep and caribou. Hiking time averages about 1 mile per hour when going cross-country in this terrain.

The part of the circuit that follows Alfred Creek lies along the route of the old Chickaloon–Knik–Nelchina Trail, which provided access to gold mines on Alfred and Albert creeks before there was a Glenn Highway. In the early 1900s, Alfred Creek was traveled by prospectors coming from Knik Arm by way of Chitna Pass (see trip 48). Gold was discovered on Alfred Creek in 1911, but prospectors were also going beyond Alfred to Albert and Crooked creeks. When the price of gold was deregulated in the mid-1970s, mining activity began again and affected both Squaw Creek and Alfred Creek valleys.

The Circuit

Starting at Squaw Creek is recommended because of wonderful views of the Chugach Mountains at trip's end. Take the Glenn Highway to mile 118.5, turn west (uphill) onto the old Glenn, and drive 800 feet to a trailhead parking area (mile 118.4, old Glenn; elevation 3,245 feet). Walk the old Glenn west to a gravel pit north of the road at mile 117.6. An ATV trail (known as Meekino Trail) begins at the back right (northeast) side of the pit. Follow this sometimes-wet trail over the toe of Gunsight Mountain and down into the Squaw Creek valley at 2,700 feet, about 3 miles. Find good camping in another mile in spruce woods just across Gunsight Creek.

From the spruce woods campsite, either follow the ATV trail through a swampy area or stay in the spruce woods and parallel Squaw Creek. After a little less than a mile, head for the creek and cross it (usually no problem—about a foot deep). Then head straight uphill to a dirt road (Squaw Creek road) that parallels the creek on a bench above it. Follow this road west (left) about 2 miles. When it descends to the level of Squaw Creek, look for an ATV trail on the right. It is about 200 yards before the road crosses Squaw Creek for the first time. There is more than one trail; if in doubt, follow the road to the first crossing of Squaw Creek and walk back to the trail.

Follow the ATV trail uphill and left (west) through brush onto a bench. Leave the trail at its high point, before it starts downhill. Strike out cross-country, heading for the pass between two bumps (locally known as Twin Peaks) that separate Squaw Creek valley from Caribou Creek valley. From here to Alfred Creek (1) there is no trail, but look for game trails through the brush. Stay high (elevation about 3,200 feet) while contouring around northern Twin Peak. There is limited camping on this slope, as flat places are hard to find (but not impossible). Water is also difficult to find, as some streams are underground in spots. Listen for water.

This 5-mile trek around the western end of Syncline Mountain is the most difficult part of the trip because of brush with only intermittent

Campsite overlooking Caribou Creek, July (Photo: Gayle Nienhueser)

game trails to follow. Near the base of the northwest side of Syncline Mountain a plateau at about 3,150 feet elevation overlooks Alfred Creek. Head for the plateau and a mining road that cuts across it. The road leads to a mining operation near the confluence of Sawmill and Alfred creeks (elevation 2,900 feet). Avoid the mine buildings, which are private property, and continue up Alfred Creek.

It is possible to hike from Squaw Creek valley to Alfred Creek valley on an ATV trail that parallels Caribou Creek (2) instead of crossing the mountain slope. This alternate route is about 3 miles longer, requires about ten crossings of Squaw Creek, and offers much easier walking except for the creek crossings. To take this route, continue on Squaw Creek road and follow it almost to Caribou Creek, about 2 miles beyond the first place the road crosses Squaw Creek. The crossings are easy, especially if stream-crossing shoes are used and not changed until after the last crossing. Just before a good, well-used campsite in spruce woods on the north side of the road (about ¼ mile before Caribou Creek), an ATV trail goes straight up a steep hill. A slightly less steep alternate trail is immediately to the left. Once up the hill, this trail offers good, easy walking for much of the way, passing through delightful meadows. It also goes through some very wet areas. After about 2½ miles, this trail intersects the Alfred Creek road. Turn right and follow this road until it turns toward the Alfred Creek canyon. Instead, head for the plateau mentioned earlier. It should be possible to find a game trail. Once on the plateau, pick up the mining road that leads down to the confluence of Sawmill and Alfred creeks.

The mining road cuts back and forth across Alfred Creek. Cross the stream at the first wide place, as it becomes increasingly difficult upstream. Cliffs on the south bank make continuing on that side impossible. Alfred Creek is a potentially dangerous stream, as it is at least knee-deep and very swift.

On the north side of Alfred Creek, follow the ATV trail where possible and bushwhack or follow gravel bars where there is no trail. This entire stretch has been thoroughly disturbed by mining. Once past the cliffs (about 2 miles downstream from the Pass Creek confluence) recross the stream. This crossing is easier, and an ATV trail continues on the south side to Pass Creek.

Pass Creek valley is usually easy to find as an ATV trail leads up it. In early summer finding the route may be more difficult because ice may cover the start of the trail. The ATV trail parallels a stream that comes from a broad pass (Belanger Pass). In early summer look for the stream to find the trail.

From the junction of Pass and Alfred creeks (elevation 3,400 feet) to the Glenn Highway, hiking time should be 4–5 hours (about 7 miles). The climb to Belanger Pass (4,350 feet) is gradual. The view of the Chugach Mountains during the descent from the pass is magnificent, a fitting climax to the trip (elevation loss about 1,400 feet). Respect and circumvent private property encountered where the trail over Belanger Pass joins Martin Road, 2 miles from the Glenn Highway. The trip ends at mile 123.3 of the Glenn Highway, at the junction of Martin Road and the Glenn Highway about a quarter mile east of Gunsight Mountain Lodge (marked by a "Trail" sign).

Squaw Creek road begins at mile 1.4 (from the Glenn Highway) on Martin Road It is possible to shorten the trip slightly by leaving a car on Squaw Creek road just after the intersection with Martin Road. Martin Road is rough but driveable by most cars with sufficient clearance. (Squaw Creek road is *not* driveable.) It is also possible to begin the trip at the junction of Martin Road and Squaw Creek road. The trip distance is about the same as the distance from the gravel pit at mile 117.6 on the Glenn Highway and the walking is easier. However, the trail from the gravel pit offers greater scenic variety.

Part or all of the circuit can be done on mountain bikes, using the route via the ATV trails.

The Traverse

To do the traverse over Syncline Mountain, follow the directions for the circuit to the western slope of Syncline Mountain, in the vicinity of Twin Peaks. To climb the mountain (elevation 5,471 feet), head up its southwest ridge (3). Game trails make much of the route easy (though steep) and the ridge-top walking is delightful. From the pass between the Twin Peaks to the high point at 5,471 feet is a little over 2 miles. From point 5471, a number of trips are possible. Stay high, exploring ridges and watching wildlife, returning at day's end to camp. (Camping on the ridge requires carrying water or descending from camp to find water.) Or descend via the steep north ridge (4) toward the plateau above Alfred Creek and continue the circuit around Syncline Mountain. Camp just above the plateau. This requires 4 days or an extremely long third day. Another possibility is to follow the ridge tops (5) east and north to Belanger Pass, about 7 miles (no water).

50 GUNSIGHT MOUNTAIN IN WINTER

Round trip: 7 miles
Allow 8–10 hours
High point: 6,441 feet

Total elevation gain: 3,140 feet
Best: February to April
USGS map: Anchorage D2

Alaska Division of Land

Gunsight Mountain, about 70 miles west of Glennallen, is named for the distinct notch between its two summits. The trip is excellent for all, from the experienced mountaineer to the novice just trying winter climbing. The superb panorama from the top of Gunsight, of the Wrangell, Chugach, and Talkeetna mountains, is well worth the effort. Proper winter gear, good physical condition, and, for the beginning winter mountaineer, experienced companions are necessary. Skiers will want climbing skins; traditional wooden snowshoes should be wrapped with heavy cord to provide greater traction on the steep slope. Lucky climbers may glimpse a band of caribou.

A summer climb of the peak requires some bushwhacking. The best approach in that season is via the Squaw Creek trail (trip 49); follow it to the north side of Gunsight, where the brush is lower.

For a winter climb, drive to the junction of the old and new Glenn Highways at about mile 118.5 (118 miles northeast of Anchorage). Turn west (uphill) onto the old Glenn and drive 800 feet to a trailhead and parking area at mile 118.4 on the old Glenn (elevation 3,245 feet).

Walk a short distance west to a creek that crosses the old Glenn Highway, and don skis or snowshoes. Head northwest, through light brush, up the gully of the creek, gradually climbing the ridge above the left side of the stream. Head toward the mountain, eventually veering southwest (left) toward the southeast summit (elevation 6,441 feet), the higher but easier of the two summits. Most of the climb is gradual and poses no technical problems. For the last few hundred feet, which are much steeper, skis or snowshoes will have to be cached. Lug soles and perhaps crampons will be necessary for adequate traction and edging on the way to the summit.

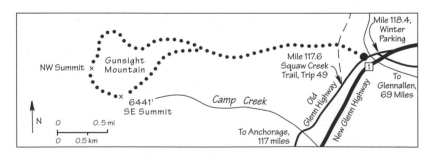

Gunsight Mountain from the Glenn Highway

A traverse of the notch and the ridge connecting the summits requires crampons and technical skill, especially in winter—it is not for beginners. Although not excessively difficult for experienced mountaineers, the route involves rappelling. To avoid the rappel, the notch can be bypassed on the back (south) side. An ascent of the northwest summit (about 6,440 feet) along the north ridge has some exposure but is also not technically difficult. If you do traverse to the northwest summit, it is possible to descend directly to your uphill trail without retreating first to the southeast summit.

Winter temperatures frequently reach minus twenty-five to minus forty degrees Fahrenheit, and wind can increase the rate at which frostbite could occur (see "Frostbite" in the Introduction). Arctic winter clothing is absolutely necessary for a midwinter climb. Be sure to have adequate footgear, such as bunny boots or backcountry ski boots with insulated super gaiters. Remember that Alaska winter days are short; watch the time. Take a flashlight, and keep its batteries warm inside your parka.

51   GULKANA RIVER

Up to 80 miles   **Best: late June to early September**
Allow 4–7 days   **USGS maps: Gulkana B3, B4, C4, D4**
River gradient: 16 feet/mile overall

National Wild River, U.S. Bureau of Land Management

Flowing through rolling, forested hill country with abundant wildlife and occasional views of the impressive Wrangell Mountains, the Gulkana River is ideal for a challenging and exciting kayak, raft, or canoe trip. Portions of the first part of the trip, from Paxson Lake to Sourdough, are difficult; the rapids in this section should be run only in a raft or by very experienced canoers or kayakers. The second part of the trip, from Sourdough Creek to Gulkana, is suitable for canoers with less experience in rapids. Splash covers for canoes and kayaks are necessary for the Paxson–Sourdough section and recommended for the Sourdough–Gulkana section. If planning a trip on the first section in June, call Paxson Lodge to be sure the ice on Paxson Lake is gone; the lake generally breaks up in mid-June.

Drive to mile 175 of the Richardson Highway (10.5 miles south of Paxson, 250 miles from Anchorage), and follow a 1.6-mile gravel road west to Paxson Lake Campground. Use the staging area next to the boat ramp for setting up and launching. The first part of the trip, from Paxson Lake Campground (1) to Sourdough Creek (6), is 45 miles and takes about 4 days by raft, 3 days by canoe or kayak. River classifications used here are those designated by the International White Water Scale (see "Boating" in the Introduction).

Paddle southwest along the shoreline to the outlet of Paxson Lake and the start of the Gulkana River. The first 3 miles of the river consist of rocky, shallow rapids; the river drops 25 feet/mile in this stretch (WW3 canoeing, difficult). After the junction with Middle Fork (2), the river is pleasant and relatively calm for 15 miles (WW2, medium).

About 18 miles from Paxson Lake a canyon begins (3) and with it

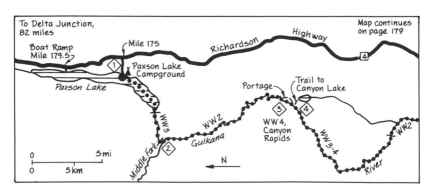

Map continues on page 179

about a quarter mile of rapids (WW4, very difficult), the most difficult water described in this book. The river is deep but has rocks; the gradient is 50 feet/mile. Boaters will be able to see and hear the beginning of the rapids in plenty of time to get to shore. Boats can be portaged for this short distance along the left bank on a trail that begins just upstream of the first white water. Before deciding to run the rapids, all boaters should stop here and hike downstream for a good look. At the first bend after the portage, a 1-mile foot trail (4) leaving the left bank leads to Canyon Lake, a pleasant side trip.

The next 8 miles of the river are rough but not excessively difficult. The remainder of the river to Sourdough (6) is WW2. About 18 miles below Canyon Rapids the West Fork (5) of the Gulkana River enters from the right.

Campsites abound along the upper river. Leave a clean campsite, dispose of human waste properly (see "Sanitation" in the Introduction) and use existing fire pits or, better, a camping stove to reduce the impact on the forests. Boil all drinking water. This is bear country, so be especially careful to keep food away from your tent (see "Moose and Bears" in the Introduction). From Paxson Lake to Sourdough, the river is designated as a National Wild River.

Caution is the word for those traveling the upper section of the river. The entire 45 miles is 1–8 miles from the road system. The frigid Alaska waters make capsizing particularly dangerous. Life jackets and wet suits or warm clothing should be worn, and at least two boats should make the trip, always maintaining sufficient distance between them to allow complete freedom of route.

From Sourdough (6) to the Gulkana exit (11), 35 miles, the river closely parallels the highway. This section generally takes 1–2 days. Actual time on the river runs 6–9 hours for canoes and kayaks and 8–12 hours for rafts. The shorter times apply when the river is high and fast. The gradient varies from 15 to 25 feet/mile, and most of this section, with pleasant pools and interesting WW2 riffles, is not difficult. A 50-yard stretch of WW3 rapids (9) is a lot of fun.

The Sourdough entrance or exit (6) is at mile 147.4 of the Richardson Highway. The final takeout (11) is at mile 127 of the Richardson

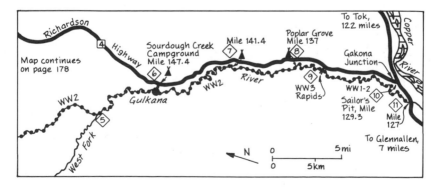

Gulkana River below Sourdough, August (Photo: Helen Nienhueser)

Highway, where the highway crosses the river. Access to the river here is over land owned by the Gulkana Village Corporation. However, boaters can take out legally just before or just after the bridge, in the Richardson Highway right-of-way, which is 300 feet wide.

Beginning just south of Sourdough Creek Campground, the river passes through Alaska Native land owned by the Ahtna Regional Corporation. Within these lands, fishing from shore above mean high water and camping are not allowed. This policy is subject to change; to determine whether it is currently in effect, contact the Ahtna Regional Corporation in Glennallen (address in the Appendix). The river is public water, and its gravel bars and the riverbed are public land.

Between Sourdough and Gulkana, boaters may camp at three public one-acre sites, marked by signs on the river. The first (7) is near mile 141.4 of the Richardson Highway; the second, Poplar Grove (8), is near mile 137; and the third, Sailor's Pit (10), is near mile 129.3. The campsites are connected to the Richardson Highway by foot trails about ¼ mile long. The trail from the highway to Poplar Grove begins in the southwest corner of a gravel pit near mile 137. Those taking a 1-day trip or wishing to avoid the WW3 rapids (9) can exit at Poplar Grove.

Along both sections of the river, watch for moose, beavers, muskrats, otter, caribou, bears, bald eagles, and red foxes. Anglers can catch lake trout, grayling, white fish, and burbot in Paxson Lake and king salmon, red salmon, rainbow trout, grayling, and white fish in the river.

52   DIXIE PASS

Wrangell–St. Elias National Park

Round trip: 21 miles	**Total elevation gain:** 3,450 feet
Hiking time: 3–4 days	**Best:** late June to early September
High point: 5,150 feet (pass), 5,770 (peak)	**USGS maps:** Valdez C1, McCarthy C8

Dixie Pass is one of the few backcountry trips in the Wrangell Mountains that can be done without an airplane. It offers the chance for a close-up view of massive, glacier-covered, 14,163-foot Mount Wrangell and of 16,390-foot Mount Blackburn. The hike follows beautiful, crystal-clear Strelna Creek along successively smaller branches until it disappears at its source just below the pass. The countryside is wild, rugged, big, and beautiful, changing from an open spruce and willow forest at lower elevations, to willow-covered gravel bars somewhat higher, to alpine tundra below the pass. Watch for bears, moose, Dall sheep, ground squirrels, and ptarmigan.

Although the hike is not long, it is not particularly easy. The short distance shown on the map is deceptive. Although there is a trail part of the way, there are no maintained trails. Part of the route has only intermittent game trails, and the hiker must choose between walking the gravel bars, crossing and recrossing the stream, or following game trails through thick willow. Map-reading and routefinding skills are necessary to ensure finding the pass. Despite this, the trip is popular with Alaska visitors because it is one of the few easily accessible routes in the Wrangell–St. Elias National Park, and the National Park Service provides information about this trip to visitors looking for backpacking opportunities.

Take the Richardson Highway to the Edgerton Cutoff (mile 82.6), and follow the Cutoff 33 miles to Chitina. At Chitina, follow signs for McCarthy. From milepost 35, just past the bridge that crosses the Copper River, drive 13.4 miles on a gravel road to Kotsina/Nugget Creek road on the left, across the road from the grass Strelna airstrip.

Follow Kotsina/Nugget Creek road 2.6 miles to the intersection of Nugget Creek and Kotsina roads. This intersection is unmarked but is easily identified by the ford of Strelna Creek on Nugget Creek road just past the intersection. Most cars should park at the intersection. Four-wheel-drive vehicles with high enough clearance can continue another 1.3 miles on Kotsina road to the Dixie Pass trailhead on the right. The trail, a narrow footpath, may not be marked. There is a small clearing across the road from the trail. The footpath is not suitable for mountain biking, but the roads make good, long bike trips possible.

The route winds through open woods of spruce and willow on a good trail for the first 2 miles. After the trail reaches Strelna Creek, it turns north to follow the creek through much denser forest. The trail in this stretch is easy to find but more difficult to walk as it is sometimes blocked by a fallen tree or heads steeply uphill to avoid a cliff.

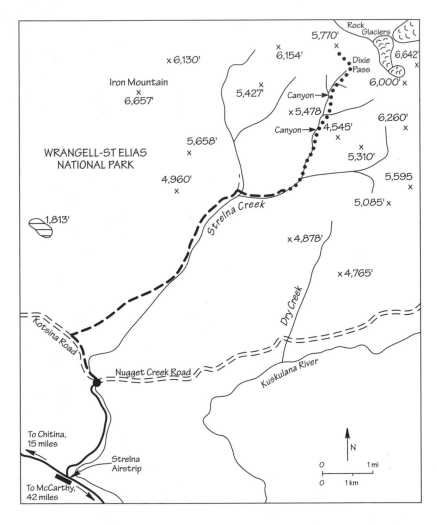

It is about 3 miles along Strelna Creek to the confluence of its west and east forks, the first major confluence on the route. The route follows the east fork. Watch carefully for the valley of the east fork. The trail does not go within sight of the confluence, and it is easy to miss it. The side valley is obvious, however, to those looking for it.

Choose a point for crossing the west fork. The creek above the confluence is generally less than knee deep and no problem to cross. Wearing boots or tennis shoes is advisable.

The route for the next 3 miles up the east fork is the most difficult part of the trip. There is a trail of sorts on the north (left) side of the creek for the first mile. Some may prefer to walk the creekbed. In either case, cross the creek to the southeast (right) bank when the trail runs into a cliff.

The route for the 2 miles beyond the initial cliff is on gravel bars or intermittent game trails through scrub willow, and it is necessary to cross the creek several times to avoid further cliffs. It may be possible to do these crossings on rocks, depending on the water level. Some of the tributary creeks are not shown on the USGS topographic map, which makes locating oneself more difficult. About a mile beyond the first tributary of the east fork that is shown on the topographic map, the creek goes through a canyon for about 100 feet. Here hikers must choose between climbing the steep hillside to get around the canyon or walking in the creek if the water level is low enough. Neither is easy. In the canyon, the water is very cold, and in one place hikers must clamber over a boulder overhung by a cliff to avoid a deep pool.

Just beyond the canyon, the valley widens into a broad gravel bar dotted with willow and laced with dwarf fireweed (elevation 3,600 feet). This is a popular campsite and could become overused. Water quality could be affected by careless toilet practices (see "Sanitation" in the Introduction).

The second tributary shown on the topographic map comes in at the north end of the gravel bar. To reach the pass (about 1½ miles farther), follow the obvious trail heading up the hill between the two forks of the creek. (The left branch of the creek leads to the pass but goes through another canyon as a waterfall.) When the trail peters out above the last willow, a choice of routes is available. To follow the ridge, head to the ridgeline on the right. This route eventually turns into a trail that leads to the pass.

An easier route requires searching for the continuing trail, which can be found in about 100 yards at nearly the same elevation. This trail heads downhill to the stream and follows it for a short distance, past the canyon of a west branch of the creek that is shown on the topographic map. The trail continues along a branch of the creek that is not shown on the map. This branch leads to the pass. Shortly, the trail disappears again at a confluence with a stream on the right, yet another stream not shown on the topographic map. At this point, pick a route to the pass. It is possible to follow the left branch of the creek to the pass or to climb the slope on either side of the left branch, eventually picking up a trail that leads to the pass.

There are beautiful views from Dixie Pass—of Strelna Creek drainage and the Chugach Mountains to the south, of Rock Creek valley and peaks reaching to 7,500 feet to the north, and, on clear days, glimpses of snowy Mount Wrangell and Mount Blackburn. But the best views by far are those from peak 5770, a short climb along the ridge to the northeast. From here the view of the huge white glaciated mass of Mount Wrangell is unforgettable.

Camping at Dixie Pass is possible, although water must be melted from snowbanks that linger most of the year on the north side or from the creek down the slope. Camping at the pass provides the option of being there when the views open up, although bad weather and wind could make camping there unpleasant. Another option is to camp part way down Rock Creek valley on the other side of the pass.

There are many good campsites on gravel bars along the entire route. Strong, fast, experienced backcountry hikers can do this trip in 2–3 days. Leisurely hikers may prefer 5 or 6 days. Allowing extra time is advisable in order to have the option to wait out bad weather and have a better chance of seeing the view.

Strelna Creek drainage, August (Photo: Helen Nienhueser)

53 KENNECOTT MINES

Round trip: 8 miles plus
   10 road miles
Hiking time: 1 or 2 days
High point: 6,050 feet

Total elevation gain: 4,700 feet
Best: June to September
USGS maps: McCarthy B5, B6, C5

Wrangell–St. Elias National Park

Historic buildings of the Kennecott Copper Corporation and nearby once-boisterous town of McCarthy sit quietly beside the Kennicott Glacier. High above, on precipitous mountain slopes, mines once disgorged precious blue-green ore onto aerial trams for transporting to the mill 4,500 feet below. Abandoned roads leading up to two of the mines, Bonanza and Jumbo, are trails into history.

The Kennecott copper deposit, which became the Bonanza Mine, was reportedly found in 1900 by two prospectors looking for a horse pasture. They mistook the distant outcropping of malachite (copper carbonate) for green grass. Nearby Jumbo Mine tapped the largest deposit in the area, producing 70,000 tons of 70 percent copper ore (with twenty ounces of silver per ton). The entire production of the Kennecott mines assayed an average of 13 percent copper. A honeycomb of more than 70 miles of layered tunnels connects the Erie, Jumbo, Bonanza, and Mother Lode mines. When the rich veins played out and the mines closed in 1938, the towns died. Through the years, Alaskans who prefer a more remote lifestyle have been reclaiming the settlements.

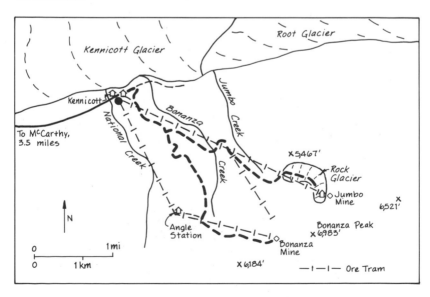

Jumbo Mine buildings, August

Drive to mile 82.6 of the Richardson Highway, turn east onto Edgerton Highway, and continue 33 miles to Chitina (254 miles from Anchorage). Expect no gas or groceries beyond here. Follow the main road through Chitina and cross the Copper River on a massive bridge. The 59-mile, single-lane, primitive gravel road ahead follows the bed of the old Copper River and Northwestern Railroad, which carried ore from Kennicott to Cordova from 1911 to 1938. The road is not recommended for large camper vehicles or trailers. Allow 2½ hours to drive the rough road, and beware of flat tires; railroad spikes churned up by road graders are a threat. The road terminates at the Kennicott River. Although residents take vehicles across winter ice, there is no automobile bridge. Park at the river, for a fee, or park at a National Park campground ½ mile before the river and walk the last bit. The primitive, walk-in campground is free. There is no official water source, but there is a spring that comes out of the hill behind the camp sites. To reach McCarthy and Kennicott, cross the Kennicott River on footbridges. Rent bicycles or arrange commercial raft trips at the river.

After crossing the Kennicott River, follow the gravel road east, up a small rise to an intersection and the McCarthy/Kennicott Historical Museum, an old red railroad depot well worth a visit. The left fork of the road goes to Kennicott, 4 miles away. The right fork leads quickly into McCarthy. An alternate access to McCarthy is to fly to the airstrip, just outside of town. Planes can be chartered in the Glennallen–Gulkana area, or take the Wednesday or Friday mail plane, making arrangements through the air charter operator (address in the Appendix).

Be sure to visit the McCarthy Lodge, built in the early 1900s, full of relics and old photographs; meals, drinks, and showers are available. The Kennicott Glacier Lodge in Kennicott is of recent construction; it also offers meals and drinks. Ask about the two spellings of Kennicott. Please camp near the Kennicott River. Clear Creek, which you cross as you walk into McCarthy, supplies drinking water to the residents; be careful not to contaminate it. Please remember that *all* structures and land in McCarthy and some in Kennicott are privately owned—do not enter buildings, take relics, or use old lumber for firewood.

To reach the mines, walk or bicycle the road north from the museum to Kennicott or contact the McCarthy lodge for a ride (charge). In Kennicott, cross the bridge over National Creek and proceed on flat ground and on the main street through town. Follow this road about 5 minutes beyond the end of town. At the only Y in the road, go right, and switchback uphill toward the mines (the left fork parallels the glacier and is a wonderful trail in itself). This route comes close to the top of the mill building, which makes a nice overlook. Continue up the main route toward the mines.

After about an hour of steady but leisurely climbing, as the road bears right, an obscure, mostly overgrown, hard-to-find trail goes left through the alders. The trail leads to Jumbo Mine, high in a cirque at 5,800 feet. The main road continues to the tram angle station and Bonanza mine, a good alternative if you miss the trail.

The Jumbo Mine trail, an old road that is quite walkable, crosses Bonanza Creek (good campsite) in less than a mile. Leave brush behind at 3,700 feet and by 4,700 feet follow the trail up a massive rock glacier. Water and a campsite are at the lower end of the glacier. Follow the old road all the way up the rock glacier as it bears right into the cirque below Bonanza Peak (elevation 6,983 feet).

To reach Bonanza Mine (elevation 5,950 feet), instead of taking the Jumbo Mine trail, continue up the main road. At an intersection near the tram, take the left fork; the right-hand trail leads to a privately owned cabin at the angle station. The buildings at the Bonanza Mine are mostly collapsed, but the scenery is well worth the climb.

Because the slope faces south, both climbs can be very hot on a sunny day. Carry plenty of water with you.

54 WORTHINGTON GLACIER OVERLOOK

Round trip: 2 miles	**Total elevation gain: 1,200 feet**
Hiking time: 2–3 hours	**Best: late June to September**
High point: 3,400 feet	**USGS map: Valdez A5**

National Natural Landmark, Alaska Division of Parks and Outdoor Recreation

Enter the lofty mountain realm of sculptured blue glacier ice. Climb a steep but easy trail to look deep into the crevasses of Worthington Glacier all the while standing on firm ground near soft green meadows. This charming alpine trail near Thompson Pass is a perfect leg-stretcher that gives a hint of the thrill of mountaineering.

Don't let cloudy or misty weather cancel the hike; the blue of the ice is more intense on gray days, and the mountains are more mysterious. This glacial landscape is recognized as a National Natural Landmark.

To reach the trail, drive to mile 28.7 of the Richardson Highway (273 miles from Anchorage, 33 miles from Valdez). Follow a side road west to the Worthington Glacier State Recreation Site parking lot. At this printing, the area was scheduled for construction, with a new shelter and a new wheelchair-accessible trail (an 1,800-foot loop) for viewing the glacier. The longer hiking trail alongside the glacier will still begin at the back of the parking area (elevation 2,200 feet) and not at the shelter. Up the trail to the left of the glacier, near the icefalls, stands a prominent gray knob, a good destination for skilled hikers. Those less skilled will enjoy climbing the first part of the trail.

Walk west up the moraine, climbing to its crest. On a sunny day, a meadow about halfway to the gray knob is a fine spot for a picnic. If children are along, watch that they don't approach the cliffs above the glacier. Carry water with you.

The more adventurous can continue to parallel the glacier edge, climbing the moraine as far as is comfortable. The trail is frequently exposed, requiring sure footing and boots with good traction. On rainy days, particularly, the moraine can be slippery; a fall could be serious, perhaps fatal. However, with caution, this little hike is one of the most delightful in south-central Alaska.

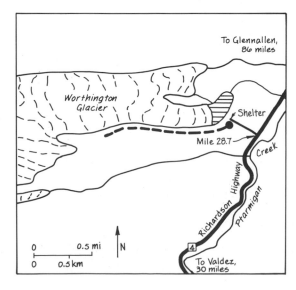

Walking on the glacier itself should be undertaken only by trained and properly equipped mountaineers.

Camp at Blueberry Lake State Recreation Site, at mile 24 of the Richardson Highway. If the grade seems too steep at Worthington, look for a flatter but unmarked trail at the back of the Blueberry Lake campground loop. It leads to a valley overlook along an old telegraph line. The whole Thompson Pass area offers good, easy hiking above timberline on heather and smooth bedrock. The area is exceptionally scenic in autumn when tiny tundra leaves burn a brilliant red.

Worthington Glacier, August (Photo: Helen Nienhueser)

SOLOMON LAKE

Round trip: 3.8 miles
Hiking time: 2–3 hours
High point: 725 feet

Total elevation gain: 750 feet
Best: June to mid-October
USGS map: Valdez A7 SE

Alaska Energy Authority

For a novel hike that combines the best of nature with interesting high technology, try the trip to Solomon Lake near Valdez.

Solomon Lake is a large reservoir that sits behind a rock-fill dam, but the dam does little to diminish the lake's green, glacial beauty. Above the lake to the east is the 3,400-foot horn of Sugarloaf Mountain, an impressively steep hunk of rock jutting up between Solomon and Abercrombie creeks. Across the waters of Port Valdez, the rugged

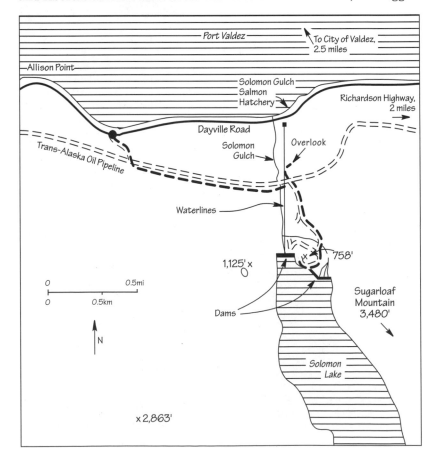

Chugach Mountains that rise above the city of Valdez make for fine photography.

The peaks give a sense of wilderness. But besides the dam, this hike is also the setting for two big water pipelines that feed a hydroelectric plant, and it coincides with the final mile of the trans-Alaska oil pipeline. The hiking route leaves the oil pipeline corridor right at pipeline milepost 798, providing the awesome impression of a strip of ground cleared across Alaska for 798 continuous miles from Prudhoe Bay to this point. The trail itself, its interpretive signs and general maintenance, are part of the hydroelectric project, and establishing the route was a permit requirement of the federal government.

To reach the trailhead, drive to mile 2.9 of the Richardson Highway, and turn southwest on Dayville Road. Note that mile 0 of the Richardson Highway is at the *old* Valdez townsite, and if you are coming from Valdez, Dayville Road is actually 6.6 miles from Meals Avenue at the city's edge. Drive about 3.7 miles on Dayville Road, a mile beyond the hydroelectric powerhouse and the Solomon Gulch Salmon Hatchery, to the trailhead (marked) on the left at an elevation of about 30 feet. A couple of free parking spaces are designated for trail users. Other parking is available along the road near the trailhead and from there to Allison Point; the City of Valdez may require a fee for these.

The walking route follows broad maintenance roads all the way to Solomon Lake. It begins by winding uphill through beautiful forest. After about 220 feet of elevation gain, it intersects the oil pipeline (buried). Go left and follow the pipeline route over gently rising terrain. Don't be tempted to hike to Prudhoe Bay; the pipeline corridor is open to the public for less than a mile—to pipeline milepost 798. At this point, just beyond the water pipelines, the hiking route goes right on a quiet maintenance road (marked). At about the same point, a spur trail to the left (also marked) leads several hundred feet and up a hill to an overlook. This provides superb views both across the water and uphill to Sugarloaf Mountain. The view is well-worth the short detour. On the main route, once away from the oil pipeline, there are two forks to the right. The first leads back to the waterlines and a dead-end. The second leads to the base of the main dam. Stay left to reach the tops of the dams (there are actually two dams holding back the lake, elevation 690 feet) and more good views.

The trailhead area has plenty of interesting things to do after the hike, or instead of the hike if the weather is bad. The hatchery and hydroelectric powerhouse offer self-guided tours. Just a little farther along Dayville Road is the terminus of the oil pipeline, built on the site of Fort Liscum. Founded in 1900, the fort existed before Valdez did, and its men opened a wagon road and established a telegraph line into interior Alaska. Alyeska Pipeline Service Company offers tours of the terminal area. Allison Point, between the trailhead and the pipeline terminus, is known for its salmon fishing.

For a shorter, flatter walk, ask in Valdez for directions to Mineral Creek, where there is an easy hike (2 miles round trip) to the remnants of the old Smith Mill, a crushing plant for gold ore. Or, near Thompson Pass outside of Valdez, try a flat but spectacular walk with dry footing (1.5 miles round trip) along an unmarked but obvious trail from the back of the Blueberry Lake State Recreation Site campground.

View across Solomon Lake, September (Photo: John Wolfe Jr.)

APPENDIX

Time of Year

Each summer trip is listed by the month the route generally is snow-free enough for use. Conditions vary greatly from year to year.

APRIL

2 Homer Beach Walk
10 Mount Marathon, Race Point runners' trail
24 Bird Ridge
27 Table Rock on McHugh Lake Trail
28 Turnagain Arm Trail

MAY

1 Grewingk Glacier Lake
3 Swan Lake and Swanson River Canoe Routes (late May)
4 Hidden Creek and Kenai River trails
5 Skilak Lookout
7 Kenai River
8 Russian Lakes
10 Race Point hikers' trail
13 Ptarmigan Lake
15 Caribou Creek (cabin) on Resurrection Pass Trail
15 Trout, Juneau, and Swan Lakes (cabins) on Resurrection Pass Trail
17 Hope Point
18 Gull Rock
20 Byron Glacier View
21 Winner Creek Gorge (late May)
25 Indian Valley
27 Overlook and McHugh Peak on McHugh Lake Trail
33 Near Point
34 Rendezvous Peak
36 The Perch
38 Thunder Bird Falls
42 Lazy Mountain
46 Nancy Lake Canoe Trails

JUNE

1 Alpine Ridge Trail
6 Fuller Lakes
6 Skyline Trail from Fuller Lakes
8 Russian Lakes–Cooper Lake Trail
8 Resurrection River Trail
9 Crescent and Carter Lakes

10 Mount Marathon
11 Exit Glacier, Harding Icefield Trail
12 Lost Lake (late June)
14 Johnson Pass
15 Resurrection Pass Trail System
23 Crow Pass (mid-June)
23 Crow Pass to Eagle River traverse (mid-June)
25 Ship Creek to Indian
26 Falls Creek
27 McHugh and Rabbit Lakes
29 Flattop
30 The Ramp
31 Williwaw Lakes
32 Wolverine Peak
33 Tikishla Peak and North Fork Campbell Creek
35 Eagle Lake (South Fork Eagle River)
35 Eagle River Overlook
37 Round Top and Black Tail Rocks
39 Twin Peaks Trail, to brushline
40 Bold Peak Valley
41 Pioneer Ridge
48 Hicks Creek–Chitna Pass
49 Syncline Mountain
51 Gulkana River
52 Dixie Pass
53 Kennecott Mines
54 Worthington Glacier Overlook (late June)
55 Solomon Lake

JULY

16 Palmer Creek Lakes
39 East Twin Pass
42 Matanuska Peak
43 Reed Lakes
45 Craigie Creek
47 Peters Hills
50 Gunsight Mountain in summer

WINTER

Some trips are more difficult in winter. See text for details.

2 Homer Beach Walk
3 Swan Lake and Swanson River Canoe Trails (ski touring)
4 Hidden Creek and Kenai River trails

8 Cooper Lake to Upper Russian Lake
9 Crescent Lake via Carter Lake
11 Exit Glacier Road ski tour to glacier
12 Lost Lake
14 Johnson Pass trailhead areas
15 Resurrection Pass Trail, Hope to Sterling Highway
19 Turnagain Pass Ski Tour
19 Turnagain Pass: Tincan Ridge or Sunburst valley
20 Bear Valley Ski Tour
21 Winner Creek Gorge
21 "Moose Meadows" cross-country ski trails
22 Glacier Creek Ski Tour
24 Bird Ridge (hiking)
25 Indian Valley
25 Ship Creek to Indian
28 Turnagain Arm Trail (skiing or hiking)
29 Flattop
30 The Ramp (to Ship Lake Pass)
31 Williwaw Lakes
31 Middle Fork Loop Ski Trail
32 Wolverine Peak
33 Near Point Trail
34 Rendezvous Peak
35 Eagle Lake (South Fork Eagle River)
36 The Perch
37 Round Top and Black Tail Rocks
43 Archangel Road near Reed Lakes trailhead
44 Hatcher Pass Ski Tour
44 Independence Mine Bowl, Microdot Ridge, April Bowl
46 Nancy Lake (skating, skiing)
48 Hicks Creek, either trailhead
49 Syncline Mountain
50 Gunsight Mountain

Length of Trip

Driving time is not considered in trip length.

SHORT TRIPS (HALF-DAY OR LESS)

Kenai Peninsula

1 Grewingk Glacier Lake (from campground at Rusty's Lagoon)

2 Homer Beach Walk
4 Hidden Creek Trail
5 Skilak Lookout
6 Lower Fuller Lake
8 Lower Russian Lake
9 Carter Lake
9 Crescent Creek, lower bridge
10 Mount Marathon, Race Point runners' trail
11 Exit Glacier, trails at toe of glacier
13 Ptarmigan Lake, west end
14 Bench Creek bridge on Johnson Pass Trail
15 Juneau Falls on Resurrection Pass Trail
16 Palmer Creek Lakes
17 Hope Point, first mile
19 Turnagain Pass Ski Tour

Portage to Potter

20 Byron Glacier View
21 Winner Creek Gorge
21 "Moose Meadows" cross-country ski trails
22 Glacier Creek Ski Tour
23 Monarch Mine on Crow Pass Trail
23 Crow Pass
24 Bird Ridge
26 Table Rock or overlook on McHugh Lake Trail
28 Turnagain Arm Trail

Anchorage Bowl

29 Flattop
30 Powerline Pass on mountain bikes
32 Wolverine Peak route to brushline
33 Near Point
34 Rendezvous Peak

North of Anchorage

36 The Perch
38 Thunder Bird Falls
39 Twin Peaks Trail, to brushline
44 Hatcher Pass, to the pass and back
44 Hatcher Pass, Independence Mine Bowl
44 Hatcher Pass, Microdot Ridge
45 Craigie Creek, Dogsled Pass (need four-wheel-drive)

Appendix

DAY TRIPS THAT MAKE GOOD OVERNIGHTS

Kenai Peninsula

Other Areas

OVERNIGHT TRIPS

These are in addition to the preceding "Day Trips That Make Good Overnights."

TRIPS OF 3 DAYS OR MORE

Good Trips for Children

Trips that are more difficult but recommended for experienced children are designated by an asterisk (*).

Kenai Peninsula

Portage to Potter

Anchorage and Other Areas

54 Worthington Glacier Overlook, first ½ mile

55 Solomon Lake (steep but short)

Trips with Associated Peaks

At least 34 peaks are associated with trips in this book. The peaks are listed here by their association with a trip. Consult USGS topographic maps for other peaks that may be accessible, with longer approaches, from these routes.

Difficult peaks are designated by an asterisk (*). Some peaks are designated difficult because they involve long, tiring ascents. Some are so designated because they may require ropes and other technical equipment and should not be attempted except by trained climbers. See trip text.

Kenai Mountains

1 Grewingk Glacier and Alpine Ridge Trail (point 4050 on Alpine Ridge)

6 Fuller Lakes (Mystery Hills 3,520 feet)

10 Mount Marathon, Race Point (Race Point 3,022 feet, Marathon Mountain* 4,063 feet)

12 Lost Lake (Mount Ascension* 5,710 feet)

17 Hope Point (Hope Point 3,706 feet)

19 Turnagain Pass Ski Tour (Tincan Ridge* point 3900)

Chugach Mountains

24 Bird Ridge (point 3505)

26 Falls Creek (South Suicide Peak* 5,005 feet)

27 McHugh and Rabbit Lakes (Ptarmigan Peak* 4,880 feet, McHugh Peak 4,301 feet)

29 Flattop (Flattop Mountain 3,510 feet)

30 The Ramp (The Ramp 5,240 feet, The Wedge 4,660 feet)

31 Williwaw Lakes (Mount Williwaw* 5,445 feet)

32 Wolverine Peak (Wolverine 4,455 feet)

33 Near Point and Tikishla Peak (Near Point 3,000 feet, Knoya Peak 4,600 feet, Tikishla Peak* 5,150 feet)

34 Rendezvous Peak (Rendezvous 4,050 feet)

35 Eagle Lake (Cantata Peak* 6,410 feet, Mount Calliope* 6,810 feet, Eagle Peak* 6,955 feet)

37 Round Top and Black Tail Rocks (Round Top 4,755 feet, Black Tail Rocks 4,446 feet, Vista Peak 5,412 feet)

39 East Twin Pass (East Twin Peak* 5,873 feet)

40 Bold Peak Valley (Bold Peak* 7,522 feet)

41 Pioneer Ridge (Pioneer Peak* 6,398 feet)

42 Lazy Mountain and McRoberts Creek (Lazy Mountain 3,720 feet, Matanuska Peak* 6,119 feet)

Talkeetna Mountains

48 Hicks Creek–Chitna Pass (Monarch Peak* 7,108 feet)

49 Syncline Mountain (Syncline 5,417 feet)

50 Gunsight Mountain in winter (Gunsight 6,441 feet)

Trips with Associated Mountain Bike Routes

2 Homer Beach Walk

8 Russian Lakes Trail

8 Russian Lakes Trail System: Cooper Lake Trail

9 Crescent Creek Trail

9 Carter Lake Trail

13 Ptarmigan Lake: the Falls Creek trail

14 Johnson Pass Trail

15 Resurrection Pass Trail

16 Palmer Creek Lakes: access road

18 Gull Rock

30 Powerline Trail

33 Near Point Trail

40 Lakeside Trail

43 Reed Lakes: access roads

45 Craigie Creek: access road

Trips Accessible from Public Transportation

The following trips may be reached by bus, train, ferry, or scheduled air service, although daily or year-round service may not be available. If an additional short distance by road must be traveled on foot, a trip is included; additional miles one way are noted. There may also be a trailhead shuttle service offered in the Anchorage area. Check with the public information centers listed under "Information Services."

Numbers key each trip to public transportation as follows:

(1) Bus service. Several intercity bus lines, with main offices in Anchorage, serve southcentral Alaska. Check the yellow pages of the telephone book for current services. Intercity bus services change often in southcentral Alaska as new services are established and others go out of business. Seward Bus Lines, however, has been in business for many years: Box 1338, Seward, AK 00661. Phones: Anchorage (907) 563-0800; Seward (907) 224-3608; Homer (907) 235-2252. Serves Seward, Homer, and Anchorage.

(2) Anchorage Public Transit, "The People Mover," 700 West Sixth Avenue, P.O. Box 196650, Anchorage, AK 99519-6650. Phone (907) 343-6543.

(3) Alaska Marine Highway (state ferry), 333 West Fourth Avenue, P.O. Box 102344, Anchorage, AK 99510. Phone (907) 272-4482; toll-free number: (800) 642-0066. Service between Whittier and Valdez and between Seward and Homer via Kodiak.

(4) Alaska Railroad, P.O. Box 107500, Anchorage, AK 99510-7500. Phone (907) 265-2494.

(5) Scheduled air service. See your travel agent.

(6) Backcountry Connections, P.O. Box 243, Glennallen, AK 99588. Phone (907) 822-5292 or (800) 478-5292 (in Alaska). Scheduled van service from Glennallen to McCarthy.

1 Grewingk Glacier and Alpine Ridge (1); (5); + water taxi
2 Homer Beach Walk (1); (5) + 1 mile
3 Swan Lake Canoe System (1) + shuttle by canoe rental service
4 Kenai River Trail (1)
6 Fuller Lakes (1)
6 Skyline Trail (1)
7 Kenai River (collapsible boat) (1)
8 Russian Lakes (1) + 1 mile
8 Resurrection River Trail (1) + 7.5 miles
9 Crescent Lake (1) + 3.3 miles
9 Carter Lake (1) or (4) + 3½ miles
10 Race Point (1) or (5) + 2 miles
11 Exit Glacier (1) + 7.5 miles
12 Lost Lake (1)
12 Primrose Trail (1) + 1 mile
13 Ptarmigan Lake, both trailheads (1)
14 Johnson Pass, both trailheads (1) or south trailhead (4) + 3 miles
15 Resurrection Pass, Sterling Highway trailhead (1)
15 Devil's Pass Trail (1)
15 Summit Creek Trail (1)
19 Turnagain Pass Ski Tour (1)
20 Byron Glacier (1) + 5½ miles or (4) + 6.7 miles
21 Winner Creek Gorge (1) + 3 miles

22 Glacier Creek Ski Tour (1) + 2 miles
23 Crow Pass (1) + 7.5 miles
24 Bird Ridge (1)
25 Indian Valley (1) + 1 mile
25 Powerline Trail, south end (1) + 1 mile
27 Table Rock (1)
27 McHugh Lake/Rabbit Lake (1)
28 Turnagain Arm Trail (1)
29 Flattop (2) + 2.7 miles
30 The Ramp (2) + 2.7 miles
30 Powerline Trail, north end (2) + 2.7 miles
31 Williwaw Lakes (2) + 1.6 miles
32 Wolverine Peak (2) + 1.6 miles
33 Near Point and Tikishla (2) + 1.6 miles
33 Knoya (2) + ¾ mile
34 Rendezvous Peak (1) or (2) + 7 miles

37 Round Top and Black Tail Rocks, (1) or (2) + 1 mile
38 Thunder Bird Falls (1) or (2)
42 Lazy Mountain (1) + 4 miles
46 Nancy Lake Canoe System (1) + 4.7 miles or (4) + 5½ miles
48 Hicks Creek/Chitna Pass, both trailheads (1)
49 Syncline Mountain, both trailheads (1)
50 Gunsight Mountain (1)
51 Gulkana River (collapsible boat) (1) or (1) and (6)
52 Dixie Pass (1) and (6) + 2.6 miles
53 Kennecott Mines (5) or (1) and (6)
54 Worthington (1) or (1) and (6)
55 Solomon Lake (1), (1) and (6), (3), or (5) + 2.7–9.3 miles

Information Sources

LAND MANAGERS
Alaska Department of Fish and Game

Homer Area Office
3298 Douglas Place
Homer, AK 99603-8027
(907) 235-8191

Alaska Division of Land

Southcentral Region
3601 C Street, P.O. Box 10-7005
Anchorage, AK 99510-7005
(907) 269-8552

Alaska Division of Parks and Outdoor Recreation

Chugach State Park
Potter Section House
Mile 115 Seward Highway
HC52, Box 8999
Indian, AK 99540
(907) 345-5014

Homer Ranger Station
P.O. Box 3248
Homer, AK 99603
(907) 235-7024

Kenai River Manager
P.O. Box 1247
Soldotna, AK 99669
(907) 262-5581

Matanuska-Susitna/Copper Basin Area Office
Finger Lake State Recreation Area
HC32, Box 6706
Wasilla, AK 99687
(907) 745-3975

Alaska Energy Authority

Alaska Department of Commerce and Economic Development
480 West Tudor Rd.
Anchorage, AK 99503
(907) 269-3000

Chugach National Forest

3301 C Street, Suite 300
Anchorage, AK 99503
(907) 271-2500
TDD (907) 271-2282
Cabin reservations: (800) 280-2267.
This number reaches a private company that takes reservations under contract to the Forest Service. In Maryland, it operates 9 A.M.-9 P.M. eastern time.

Glacier District Office
P.O. Box 129
Girdwood, AK 99587
(907) 783-3242

Seward District Office
P.O. Box 390
Seward, AK 99664
(907) 224-3374

Fort Richardson Military Reservation

Military Police (907) 384-0823 or
Military Fish and Wildlife Office
(907) 384-0431 (numbers to call to be
sure military land is open).

Kenai National Wildlife Refuge

P.O. Box 2139
Soldotna, AK 99669
(907) 262-7021

U.S. Bureau of Land Management

(Gulkana National Wild River)
P.O. Box 147
Glennallen, AK 99588
(907) 822-3218

Wrangell–St. Elias National Park and Preserve

Mile 105.1 Richardson Highway
P.O. Box 29
Glennallen, AK 99588
(907) 822-5235

ADDITIONAL INFORMATION
SOURCES

Ahtna Regional Corporation

Ahtna, Inc.
P.O. Box 649
Glennallen, AK 99588
(907) 822-3476

Alaska Avalanche School

Alaska Mountain Safety Center
9140 Brewsters Drive
Anchorage, AK 99516
(907) 345-3566

Alaska Department of Natural Resources Public Information Center

Frontier Building
3601 C Street, Suite 200
P.O. Box 107005
Anchorage, AK 99510-7005
(907) 269-8400

Alaska Department of Transportation and Public Facilities

P.O. Box 196900
Anchorage, AK 99519-6900
Numbers to call for highway and
road conditions:
(907) 273-6037 (recording)
(907) 269-0760 (main number,
Maintenance Division)
(907) 745-2159 (Matanuska-Susitna
District)

Alaska Division of Tourism

P.O. Box 110801-0801
Juneau, AK 99811
(907) 465-2010 (Juneau)
Ask for the "Vacation Planner," a
publication, revised annually, that
lists names, addresses, and phone
numbers of businesses and services
of interest to the traveler (e.g., car
rental, guide services), including
those offering canoe and raft trips.

Alaska Public Lands Information Center

605 West Fourth Avenue
Anchorage, AK 99501
(907) 271-2737
TDD (907) 271-2738

Alaska Railroad

See "Trips Accessible from Public
Transportation," above.

Alaska Wilderness Recreation and Tourism Association

P.O. Box 22827
Juneau, AK 99802-2827
(907) 463-3038 awrta@alaska.net

Appendix

Cooperative Extension Service
2221 East Northern Lights Boulevard #118
Anchorage, AK 99508
(907) 279-5582

Ellis Air Taxi
P.O. Box 106
Glennallen, AK 99588
(907) 822-3368
Mail plane to McCarthy from Glennallen or Anchorage

Homer Visitor Information Center
(907) 235-5300

U.S. Geological Survey
Earth Science Information Center
4230 University Drive
Anchorage, AK 99508-4664
(907) 786-7011
Alaska topographic maps, over-the-counter sales

CANOE, KAYAK, AND OUTDOOR GEAR RENTALS
The following list may not be complete; check the yellow pages for a thorough listing.

Anchorage
Adventure Cafe/Coastal Kayaking
414 K Street
Anchorage, AK 99501
(907) 276-8282
Outside Alaska: (800) 288-3134
Kayaks; mountain bikes

Recreational Equipment, Inc. (REI)
1200 West Northern Lights Boulevard
Anchorage, AK 99503
(907) 272-4565
Canoes, camping equipment

Soldotna (Kenai Peninsula)
The Fishing Hole
139B Warehouse Street
Soldotna, AK 99669
(907) 262-2290

The Sports Den
44176 Sterling Highway
Soldotna, AK 99669
(907) 262-7491

Sterling (Kenai Peninsula)
The Great Alaska Fish Camp
HCO1, Box 218
Sterling, AK 99672
(907) 262-4515
Located at Moose River takeout at mile 82 of the Sterling Highway; canoes, shuttle service

Willow (North of Anchorage)
Nancy Lake Resort
P.O. Box 114
Willow, AK 99688
(907) 495-6284
Canoes and car top carriers

Tippecanoe Rentals
P.O. Box 1175
Willow, AK 99688-1175
(907) 495-6688
Canoes available at Lynx Lake Loop trailhead and other locations

Conservation and Outdoor Organizations
Alaska Center for the Environment
519 West Eighth Avenue
Suite 201
Anchorage, AK 99501
(907) 274-3621

Alaska Conservation Foundation
750 West Second Avenue
Suite 104
Anchorage, AK 99501
(907) 276-1917

Alaska State Parks Foundation
P.O. Box 245001
Anchorage, AK 99524-5001

Arctic Bicycle Club, Mountain Bikers
P.O. Box 244302
Anchorage, AK 99524
(907) 249-9199

Knik Canoers and Kayakers
P.O. Box 101935
Anchorage, AK 99510
(907) 566-1554

Mountaineering Club of Alaska
Box 102037
Anchorage, AK 99510
Meets at 7:30 P.M. third Wednesday
of each month, Pioneer Schoolhouse,
Third Avenue and Eagle Street in
Anchorage

National Audubon Society
308 G Street, #217
Anchorage, AK 99501
(907) 276-7034

National Outdoor Leadership School
(NOLS)
P.O. Box 981
Palmer, AK 99645
(907) 745-4047

National Parks and Conservation
Association
329 F Street, #208
Anchorage, AK 99501
(907) 277-6722

Nordic Skiing Association of
Anchorage/Nordic Ski Club
203 West 15th Avenue, Suite 204
Anchorage, AK 99501-3504
(907) 276-7609
Recording: (907) 248-6667
nordski@alaska.net

Park Watch
c/o Chugach State Park
HC52, Box 8999
Indian, AK 99540
(907) 345-5014
Organizes volunteers to camp at
trailheads, thus discouraging vandals

Sierra Club
241 East Fifth Avenue, Suite 205
Anchorage, AK 99501
(907) 276-4048

The Wilderness Society
430 West Seventh Avenue,
Suite 205
Anchorage, AK 99501
(907) 272-9453

INDEX

About the Authors

HELEN NIENHUESER, originally from Pennsylvania, has lived and hiked in Alaska since 1959. An honorary lifetime member of the Mountaineering Club of Alaska, she lives in Anchorage, where she was formerly a land planner for the Alaska Department of Natural Resources. Now retired, she spends her spare time exploring Alaska's backcountry.

JOHN WOLFE JR. has been scrambling in the peaks of southcentral Alaska since he was a small child. He has guided on Denali (Mount McKinley) and has been a children's environmental education instructor. He is now an editor and environmental planner for an Anchorage consulting firm.

NANCY SIMMERMAN is a professional outdoor photographer and author specializing in Alaska subjects. She is the author of *Alaska's Parklands: The Complete Guide* and *Alaska II*, a large-format photographic essay.

THE MOUNTAINEERING CLUB OF ALASKA, founded in 1958, is a nonprofit outdoor organization with the following purposes:

To promote the enjoyment of hiking, climbing, and exploration of the mountains;

Cultivation of mountain-climbing skills and techniques;

To teach and encourage safety;

To assist in the prevention of waste and unnecessary destruction of the natural scene.

The Mountaineering Club meets at 7:30 P.M. on the third Wednesday of every month at the Pioneer Schoolhouse, 3rd and Eagle Streets in downtown Anchorage. New members and guests are welcome. The club sponsors classes and a regular schedule of hikes and climbs. For more information contact:

Mountaineering Club of Alaska
Box 102937
Anchorage, Alaska 99510

THE MOUNTAINEERS, founded in 1906, is a nonprofit outdoor activity and conservation club, whose mission is "to explore, study, preserve, and enjoy the natural beauty of the outdoors...." Based in Seattle, Washington, the club is now the third-largest such organization in the United States, with 15,000 members and five branches throughout Washington State.

The Mountaineers sponsors both classes and year-round outdoor activities in the Pacific Northwest, which include hiking, mountain climbing, ski-touring, snowshoeing, bicycling, camping, kayaking and canoeing, nature study, sailing, and adventure travel. The club's conservation division supports environmental causes through educational activities, sponsoring legislation, and presenting informational programs. All club activities are led by skilled, experienced volunteers, who are dedicated to promoting safe and responsible enjoyment and preservation of the outdoors.

The Mountaineers Books, an active, nonprofit publishing program of the club, produces guidebooks, instructional texts, historical works, natural history guides, and works on environmental conservation. All books produced by The Mountaineers are aimed at fulfilling the club's mission.

If you would like to participate in these organized outdoor activities or the club's programs, consider a membership in The Mountaineers. For information and an application, write or call The Mountaineers, Club Headquarters, 300 Third Avenue West, Seattle, Washington 98119; (206) 284-6310.

Send or call for our catalog of more than 300 outdoor books:
The Mountaineers Books
1001 SW Klickitat Way, Suite 201
Seattle, WA 98134
1-800-553-4453